Creeds in Competition

OTHER BOOKS BY LEO PFEFFER

CHURCH, STATE, AND FREEDOM

LIBERTIES OF AN AMERICAN

Creeds in Competition

A CREATIVE FORCE IN AMERICAN CULTURE

BY LEO PFEFFER

GREENWOOD PRESS, PUBLISHERS
WESTPORT, CONNECTICUT

Library of Congress Cataloging in Publication Data

Pfeffer, Leo, 1910-
  Creeds in competition.

   Reprint of the ed. published by Harper, New York.
  Includes index.
    1. United States--Religion. 2. Religion and
state--United States. I. Title.
[BL2530.U6P44 1978]   291.1'77'0973   78-2308
ISBN 0-313-20349-0

Copyright © 1958 by Leo Pfeffer

Reprinted with the permission of Harper & Row, Publishers, Inc.

Reprinted in 1978 by Greenwood Press, Inc.
51 Riverside Avenue, Westport, CT. 06880

Printed in the United States of America

10 9 8 7 6 5 4 3 2 1

TO RABBI IRVING MILLER

ma'sekha y'shabḥukha

Contents

1. COMPETITION IN THE MARKET OF CULTURE   1

    A SHORT HISTORY OF CHRISTMAS   1

    THE RELEVANCE OF CHRISTMAS   3

    THE THEME OF THIS BOOK   6

    THE BACKGROUND OF COMPETITION   8

    ARE THERE PROTESTANT, CATHOLIC, AND JEWISH
        POSITIONS?   12

    IS COMPETITION GOOD OR BAD?   15

    WHAT IS AMERICAN ABOUT THE EXPERIMENT?   17

2. THE COMPETITORS AND THEIR WARES   19

    PREJUDICE OR POWER?   19

    NEW ENGLAND CALVINISM   25

    ANGLICANISM   26

PROTESTANT DISSENT   27

SECULAR HUMANISM   29

ROMAN CATHOLICISM   30

JUDAISM   34

3. RELIGION AND THE STATE   36

RELIGIOUS LIBERTY IN CATHOLIC DOGMA, HISTORY,
    AND PRACTICE   36

THE CATHOLIC REPLY   38

THE FAITHS AND FREEDOM   41

SEPARATION OF CHURCH AND STATE   43

THE MEANING OF THE NO-ESTABLISHMENT CLAUSE   46

CHURCH AND STATE IN CATHOLICISM   50

SEPARATION AND AMERICAN JEWRY   53

THE PROTESTANT DILEMMA   55

4. GOD AND THE SCHOOLS   57

PROTESTANTISM AND PUBLIC EDUCATION   57

AMERICAN JEWRY AND THE PUBLIC SCHOOLS   59

CATHOLICISM AND COMMON EDUCATION   60

THE SECULARIZATION OF THE SCHOOLS   64

THE LAW, THE CONSTITUTION, AND THE MCCOLLUM
    CASE   66

AFTERMATH OF MCCOLLUM—A NEW ALLIANCE?   69

5. PRIVATE SCHOOLS AND THE PUBLIC PURSE 75

    THE CATHOLIC PAROCHIAL SCHOOL 75

    NON-CATHOLIC PRIVATE SCHOOLS 77

    CONS AND PROS OF PAROCHIAL EDUCATION 79

    PRIVATE SCHOOLS AND THE LAW 82

    PUBLIC FUNDS FOR PAROCHIAL SCHOOLS?—THE
        CATHOLICS' CASE 85

    PROTESTANT OPPOSITION 88

    THE JEWISH POSITION 89

    INDIRECT AID AND THE EVERSON CASE 90

6. MORALS, CENSORSHIP, AND BLUE SUNDAY 93

    OUR CHANGING MORALS 93

    AN EXPERIMENT NOBLE IN MOTIVE 96

    BINGO 99

    OBSCENITY AND CENSORSHIP 103

    BLUE SUNDAY 109

7. THE FAMILY AND THE CHILD 112

    CHURCH DOGMA AND FAMILY WELFARE 112

    BIRTH CONTROL 114

    ABORTION 117

    EUTHANASIA, STERILIZATION, ARTIFICIAL
        INSEMINATION 120

SEX EDUCATION IN THE PUBLIC SCHOOLS ... 121

DIVORCE ... 122

CHILD WELFARE ... 124

ADOPTION ... 127

8. ISSUES DOMESTIC AND FOREIGN ... 133

THE SOCIAL GOSPEL ... 133

COMMUNISM WITHIN THE GATES ... 136

CIVIL LIBERTIES ... 140

WAR, PEACE, PACIFISM, AND THE ATOM BOMB ... 142

SOVIET COMMUNISM AND THE IRON CURTAIN ... 145

AMBASSADOR TO THE VATICAN ... 148

ISRAEL, ZIONISM, AND THE ARABS ... 149

9. THE CONSEQUENCES OF COMPETITION ... 153

THE THESIS RESTATED ... 153

COMPETITION AND CONFLICT ... 155

THE USES OF CONFLICT ... 158

RULES OF FAIR COMPETITION ... 160

THE CHURCH IN POLITICS ... 163

COMPETITION AND CHANGE ... 165

COMPETITION AND AMERICA'S FUTURE ... 167

INDEX ... 169

Creeds in Competition

1. COMPETITION IN THE MARKET OF CULTURE

A SHORT HISTORY OF CHRISTMAS

It was a criminal offense to celebrate Christmas in colonial New England. Although the American Puritans did not go as far as the Puritans of Old England, whose Parliament in 1644 not only prohibited all festivities on December 25 but ordered that day to be kept as a fast, they did, nevertheless, take stern measures against any misguided person who celebrated what they deemed the ill-begotten offspring of paganism and popery. If fasting was not required by law at Massachusetts Bay, participation in the feasting, pomp, and revelry that had characterized the observance of Christmas in the Old World was likely to land the celebrant in the stocks or at the whipping post.

By the turn of the nineteenth century, Christmas had become legal and its observance respectable (although even during the nineteenth century in Boston one could experience the displeasure of the community or lose his job for observing the holiday). St. Nicholas, brought over from Holland by the settlers of New Amsterdam, became a national symbol not of any particularly saintly attributes, but of the merriment, good will, and camaraderie with which the new republic was overflowing in the era of good-feeling. Indeed, by the middle of the nineteenth century Christmas had become a national holiday with little more conscious Christian religious significance than Thanksgiving. Certainly, it was not Christ's mass that was observed. Christmas carols, of course, were sung and their words hailed the Nativity. Yet the carolers and their listeners hardly experienced the religious feelings inspired by church hymns. What were

1.

being sung were quaint Elizabethan and Continental winter songs with little more religious content than "Jingle Bells."

Christmas, like Thanksgiving, had become a family holiday with the family feast the principal, or one of the principal, events of the celebration. In fact, the traditional food of the Christmas dinner was substantially the same as that at Thanksgiving, with goose sometimes substituted for turkey as the peculiar delight of the day. There were differences, to be sure. Christmas was more a children's holiday, while Thanksgiving belonged to the grown-ups. Christmas was merry; Thanksgiving was solemn. By the end of the nineteenth century the Christmas tree, and with it gifts for the children, had become an indispensable part of the festivities. However, despite differences in detail, Christmas was certainly hardly more a Christian holy day than was Thanksgiving.

In the mad decade of the return to normalcy after World War I, a Dionysian element crept into the Christmas celebration, at least in urban areas. The office party, at which first "bathtub gin" and later, in the thirties, legal liquor was freely imbibed, preceded the evening feast at home. Toward mid-century, the giving of gifts, which had spread from children to persons of all ages, and the exchange of elaborate cards became among the most important rituals of the Christmas celebration. The Christmas season trade played a major role in the American economy, particularly in the consumers' goods industry. The claims of the commercial interests in the Christmas holiday were recognized as valid by the Federal government, which considerately advanced Thanksgiving Day from its traditional last Thursday in November to the fourth Thursday so as to leave adequate time for Christmas shopping in those years in which November has five Thursdays.

It was not only the department stores that ushered in the Christmas season the day after Thanksgiving. Almost from the fourth Friday in November public streets and parks began to be decorated with Christmas trees and Stars of Bethlehem.

In more recent years, elaborate mangers, crèches, illuminated crosses and similar sacramentals of Christmas were added in public displays. In the public schools preparations for the Christmas pageant, often centering around an elaborate Nativity play, started immediately after Thanksgiving. The demand to "put Christ back into Christmas" was heard with increasing frequency and intensity. The televised celebration of the mass became a regular concomitant of

Christmas. With it too came the performance on television of plays and the exhibition of films based on the life of Jesus.

Concurrently, during the forties and fifties, a rather curious addition was made to the Christmas celebration in the public schools of many urban communities. The Jewish holiday of Hanukkah, commemorating the successful war of the Maccabees against the Seleucids in the second century before Christ, was introduced into the public schools, and joint Christmas-Hanukkah celebrations became popular. At the same time, and also in urban public schools, it was protested that Christmas celebrations had become too Christological and that a Christmas into which Christ had been put back perhaps did not belong in public education. In those schools in which there were substantial numbers of Jewish children, these protests often resulted in informal and occasionally formal directives by school officials to teachers cautioning them to avoid offending the sensitivities of Jewish children in celebrating the Christmas holiday, directives that some teachers found difficult to understand and more found difficult to follow.

THE RELEVANCE OF CHRISTMAS

What this abbreviated historical account of Christmas in America has to do with the theme of this book may perhaps best be explained by first examining the forces responsible for the various changes that Christmas has undergone. As we have seen, Calvinist Puritanism was responsible for the initial outlawing of Christmas in colonial New England. In the late eighteenth century Protestant dissent and deistic humanism combined to bring back Christmas as a national family holiday of good cheer and friendliness. In the nineteenth century the increasingly potent factor of American nationalism, illustrated by an act of Congress making the day a nation-wide legal holiday, contributed to the evolution of the American Christmas. In the early twentieth century the spirit of materialism that had sprung from the nation's rapid industrial growth extended its embrace to encompass Christmas along with almost every other aspect of communal living. The more recent pressure to restore Christ to Christmas and make of it a real Christian holy day characterized by elaborate rituals, ceremonials, and tangible sacramentals came principally from Roman Catholic sources, while conversely the resistance to these efforts, together with the coupling of Hanukkah with Christmas in the public schools, reflected Jewish influence.

Because Christmas is a major institution in American culture, its history has been outlined here to illustrate the effect of different influences on American culture. The changes they effected in Christmas have been duplicated to a substantial degree over the years in many other American cultural institutions. To trace, for example, the mutation of the Sabbath from the "blue Sunday" of New England Puritanism to the present Sunday of baseball double-headers and auto-clogged highways is to find the same influences at work in very much the same way. Similarly, Easter, beginning with its bunnies, colored eggs, and children's games, was augmented by the parade whose purpose was to mark the opening of the spring season in women and men's apparel. This trend evoked again the cry to put Christ back into Easter, as well as pressures to make Good Friday a legal holiday, the widespread televising of masses and Passion plays and films, and the erection of large crucifixes in public streets and parks. Or, in a completely different area, one might trace the development of the American educational system from the Bible schools of colonial New England to the twentieth-century combination of secular public schools and Roman Catholic parochial schools.

What is revealed by such an examination of the history in America of Christmas or Sunday or Easter or the school system (or, for that matter, our moral and criminal code, our concepts of family relations, our arts, and a variety of other aspects of American life) is, I suggest, briefly this: Our society is composed of a multiplicity of elements each of which seeks to shape the institutions of American culture according to its own scale of values. Out of this never-ending competition comes America's pluralistic culture, ever dynamic, ever changing, ever reflecting the stresses and pulls of the multifarious and contradictory elements and yet somehow coming out as a substantially harmonious orchestration of these components. This process may fairly be called creative competition.

In the shaping of American cultural patterns and values, of course, religion constitutes only one among many competing elements, or groups of elements. Indeed, as we have seen, even in the shaping of what is primarily a religious cultural institution, such as Christmas or Easter or Sunday, secular elements play a significant role. The present discussion, however, has to do with the religious competitors; non-religious competitors will enter only incidentally and only where relevant to a consideration of the religious protagonists. In short, this book is concerned with creative competition among religious cultures.

In this study I shall regard humanism as a religion along with the three major theistic faiths: Protestantism, Catholicism, and Judaism. This, I submit, is not an unreasonable inclusion. Ethical Culture is exclusively humanist but is generally considered a religion; it is, for example, included in the annual *Yearbook of American Churches* published by the National Council of Churches, and its leaders, like the clergymen of all faiths, are authorized to solemnize marriages, conduct funeral services, and perform other clerical functions. Unitarianism and Universalism, which are uniformly considered religions, are essentially humanist. Today's humanism is in large measure a descendant of eighteenth-century deism, which has frequently been treated as a religion. As will appear, humanism has often allied itself with two of the three major theistic faiths, Protestantism and Judaism, and has acted in the cultural market in the same way. For these and other reasons, convenience dictates that it be considered a religion in this book.

Principally humanism will be examined for its effects on the philosophies, ways of life, values and positions on public issues of the three major theistic faiths.

The religious protagonists—like the non-religious ones—seek to achieve their goal in a variety of ways. One is through missionary activity: if all or almost all Americans could be converted to a particular faith, American culture would be determined by the patterns and values of that faith. Another is through what its practitioners call education and its opponents call propaganda. Protestantism has sought to educate all Americans, non-Protestants as well as Protestants, on the evils of drink, and Catholicism has sought to educate all Americans on the evils of divorce. Still another way can be recognized by considering one aspect of the history of Christmas. The Puritan fathers did not content themselves with discouraging observance of Christmas among members of the Congregational Church; nor did they content themselves with discouraging observance by educating the people to the evils of Christmas. They decreed a law, applicable to all, making it a punishable offense against the government to celebrate Christmas. In the nineteenth century the law was again resorted to when Christmas was made a national holiday through the enactment by Congress of a statute declaring it to be a holiday and ordering government offices to be closed on that day. In the twentieth century extension and intensification of Christmas observance was sought by making use of the facilities of state-controlled public schools.

What is true of Christmas is equally true of the Sabbath, as the numerous Sunday laws throughout the nation testify. Current efforts to make Good Friday a legal holiday, the Eighteenth Amendment and state anti-liquor laws, anti-lottery laws, statutes making it a criminal offense to disseminate information concerning birth control —these and a multitude of other illustrations can be cited to show how religious groups attempt to translate their own cultural and moral values into law.

THE THEME OF THIS BOOK

There are three significant differences between the Puritan era and contemporary America in this respect. In the first place, the Puritan church had no secular competitors; in fact, church and state were but a single entity. Hence, the state as church automatically promulgated into secular law what it believed was needed for the salvation of the community and its citizens. But today the church is in competition with many secular forces in the community, bent on shaping society according to their own value judgments. Today the church must cope with the liquor industry in any effort to convince the community that laws prohibiting or regulating the sale of intoxicating liquors should be enacted or retained. It must cope with the medical profession in seeking the enactment of laws forbidding dissemination of birth control information. Catholic labor union members are faced with competing claims upon their loyalties when their unions urge them to vote only for candidates pledged in favor of a Child Labor Amendment, while the Catholic Church urges the defeat of that amendment. Laws urged by religious groups for the censorship of books or motion pictures are opposed by the publishing and motion picture industries, as well as by civil liberties groups, the writing profession, library associations, and other organizations.

In the second place, none of these competing forces can achieve their goals through command. Today the laws of the community are promulgated by individual citizens selected for that purpose and who are (or at least ought to be) free of control or domination from any source other than their fellow citizens who chose them to make the laws. Hence, the church, equally with its competitors, can achieve its goal only by the voluntary action of the same citizen-elected lawmakers. Where it previously commanded, the church must now induce. It must persuade the lawmakers—or, more accurately, the community they represent—that what the church urges is best for the community, and that the values the church seeks to implement through the community's laws are best for the community.

The third significant difference between colonial times and the present is in the nature of the church itself. In early colonial times the church (Congregational in New England, or Anglican in the South) was a single, undivided and all-pervasive entity. It was the sole representative of Christianity in the community as Christianity was the sole religion of and in the community. Today, the word "church" can be used properly only as a shorthand term indicating religious forces and institutions in general. The church today faces not only external but internal competition as well. Within Protestantism there is competition among the various denominations in value judgments. Methodists and Episcopalians, for example, do not see eye to eye on the desirability of laws prohibiting the manufacture or sale of intoxicating liquors. Protestantism must compete with Catholicism as to what standards and values are really implicit in Christianity and both must compete with Judaism as to what standards and values are really implicit in religion.

In sum, where the church in earlier times commanded, it must now convince. Where it earlier controlled, it must now compete. And where it earlier was a single, united force, it is now divided within itself and subject to internal as well as external competition.

Thus we come to the theme of this book. Briefly, it is a study of this internal competition, an examination of the efforts of the major religious forces to shape American culture through governmental action either in the enactment of laws or in the operation of governmental institutions, such as the public school system, the family courts, the foreign service, the civil service, the public treasury, etc. The book proposes to examine the differing positions taken by the three major faiths on issues of public importance, directly or indirectly involving the institutions of government and law, and the arguments presented by the three faiths to convince the American public of the justice and wisdom of their positions in order that those positions shall be translated into the law of the land and thus shape the culture of the American community.

THE BACKGROUND OF COMPETITION

Among the major faiths, creative competition in the arena of public issues is a comparatively recent phenomenon. The reason is fairly simple: there can be no competition without competitors. As we have seen, colonial Protestantism (in New England and in the South) had no competitors at all. Since church and state were partners, there was no need for Protestantism to justify its wares to the state. The partnership, however, was dissolved toward the end of the eighteenth century by the adoption of Federal and state constitutions separating church and state and providing for religious liberty. Thereafter, Protestantism had to compete with secular forces and institutions. But for more than a century it continued to enjoy a monopoly in the field of religion; until the second quarter of the twentieth century, Protestantism had no serious religious competitors. Insofar as American culture was influenced by religion, it was influenced by Protestantism. There were, of course, different strains within Protestantism with varying approaches to public issues. But in many major areas Protestant denominations were largely in agreement and united to influence American culture; the Prohibition experiment, the nonsectarian public educational system, and the moral code are but three illustrations. It is only recently that Roman Catholicism has become a full-fledged competitor, and even more recently that Judaism has emerged as a competing force to be contended with.

Free and effective competition in any field demands that the wares of each competitor have equal access to the market with no personal discrimination or disabilities. There can be no real competition if it is illegal to buy the wares of any but one of the competitors; and there can be no real competition if any of the competitors are jailed by the authorities or boycotted by a prejudiced community. A brief glance at the history of interreligious relationships in America reveals but a recent achievement of equality or substantial equality among the major faiths and their adherents.

Three fairly distinct periods can be discerned. The first corresponded roughly with the colonial period, in which the underlying motif was dogma or theology. The second ended at about the beginning of the second quarter of the twentieth century, and was characterized by bigotry or prejudice. The third constitutes the present period of creative competition, with its differences on public issues.

During the colonial period, Protestants were set apart from other Protestants and from Catholics, and Christians from Jews, principally if not exclusively through differences in theology. Dogma and creed were supreme in the New England church-state and only slightly less so in Anglican Virginia. The Congregational church-state was ruled by a small oligarchy who could meet the stringent theocratic qualifications for citizenship. Quakers and Catholics were barred from the colony under pain of death and every effort was made to eradicate "pestilent heresy." The extent to which dogma determined relationships in Puritan New England is indicated by the fate of Anne Hutchinson. Mrs. Hutchinson was neither a Quaker nor a Catholic, but a Congregationalist like the members of the Massachusetts Bay General Court who exiled her to her death because she persisted in preaching the obstinate heresy of a "covenant of grace" rather than the orthodox "covenant of works." In early seventeenth-century Virginia, criticism of the Trinity or of any article of the Christian faith was punishable by death, and even on the eve of the Revolutionary War, a Christian who denied the Trinity could be deprived of custody of his own children.

By the end of the eighteenth century religious dogma ceased to be patently significant in interreligious relationships. A variety of causes combined to eliminate theology as a major factor in the secular life of the community. The expanding frontier, the nationalism that emerged from the War for Independence, the secularism that came with the French Enlightenment and the French Revolution, the widespread irreligion of the last quarter of the century, and the rise of the individualistic dissenting sects that attracted the majority of those Americans who retained adherence to theistic religion—all combined to diminish the importance of differences in theological creed and dogma. Toward the end of the eighteenth century the Constitution of the new republic and those of the states all guaranteed citizens the freedom to adhere to any religious dogma or creed that appealed to their conscience. By 1833, when the last of the established churches had been separated from the state, differences in religious dogma ceased to be of avowed or direct significance in interreligious relationships. (That they continue to be of unavowed or indirect significance will become apparent in the next chapter.)

The rise of nationalism, which accelerated the elimination of dogma as a conscious factor in interreligious relationships, raised to prominence another aspect of such relationships. For nationalism brought with it bigotry and prejudice against the immigrants and aliens who congregated in the Eastern coastal cities. These were almost entirely Catholics and Jews. (The minority of Catholic immigrants who accompanied German and Scandinavian Lutheran immigrants to the Middle West were in large measure accorded equal treatment with the Protestant immigrants.) The Catholics who came from Ireland after the potato famine in the first half of the nineteenth century and those who later came from Italy and eastern Europe to build our railroads and to work our mines and mills were all the victims of the xenophobia that spread through the United States in the late nineteenth and early twentieth centuries. The large-scale immigration of Jews from eastern Europe after the pogroms and persecutions under the Russian czars subjected them to the same American xenophobia. The underlying motif of this era was bigotry and the chief anti-Catholic and anti-Jewish forces were the super-nationalists, the Know-Nothings, the Nativists, and later the Ku Klux Klan.

During the early part of this era there were widespread circulation of exposés of the evils of nunneries and confessions of ex-nuns and ex-priests. Toward its end there was similar dissemination of the Protocols of the Elders of Zion and other exposés of Jewish conspiracies to subjugate the Gentiles and control the world. These, however, were not aimed either at the dogma of Catholicism or at the religion of Judaism. They were rather the manifestations of the fear-begotten bigotry that so often meets what is alien and strange. As religions, Catholicism and Judaism had won the same equality of status with orthodox Protestantism that had earlier been accorded to dissenting Protestantism. But creative competition among religious cultures was not yet possible because Catholics and Jews had not yet achieved equality with Protestants in the American community.

The era of bigotry in interreligious relationships in the United States may be said to have come to a substantial end in 1928 for Catholics and at the end of World War II for Jews. This does not mean that there is no longer anti-Catholic prejudice or anti-Jewish discrimination in the United States. It means only that such prejudice and discrimination have ceased to be significant factors in interreligious relations. It means that by and large the American people will consider a candidate for public office on his own merits and will vote for or against him without giving substantial consideration to the fact that he is a Catholic or a Jew and that they will consider a particular public issue on its merits without giving substantial consideration to the religion of its proponent.

In view of the well-publicized anti-Catholic bigotry, particularly in the South, during the election campaign of the Catholic Alfred E. Smith in 1928, it might seem strange to suggest that that year marked the end of the era of bigotry in respect to Catholics. Yet, what was significant in 1928 was not the circulation of anti-Catholic leaflets but the fact that one of the two major political parties nominated a Catholic for the Presidency. Since the first aim of a political party is to win, it is a reasonable assumption that Smith would not have been nominated if the delegates to the Democratic Convention had not believed that his Catholicism would not constitute an insurmountable obstacle to his election. Moreover, it is a reasonable conclusion that Smith's Catholicism did not play a significant role in the final outcome of the campaign, and that had he been a Protestant he would likewise have been defeated (other things being equal). In any event, the fact that anti-Catholic bigotry is no longer significant in American community affairs is evidenced by two incidents. The first occurred during the Democratic Convention in 1956 when the strongest support for Senator John F. Kennedy, a Catholic, for the Vice-Presidential nomination came from the Southern delegations, who were almost solidly for his selection. The second took place in 1957, when a major Ku Klux Klan organization in the South opened its membership rolls to Roman Catholics.

The disappearance of anti-Jewish bigotry as a factor in public affairs is less obvious, and undoubtedly there are more vestiges of such bigotry than of anti-Catholic bigotry. Nevertheless, here too it is safe to suggest that bigotry and prejudice are no longer very important in Christian-Jewish relationships. Senator Joseph R. McCarthy, it will be remembered, carefully avoided the anti-Semitism of the Reverend Charles Coughlin and made studied efforts to show his friendliness to the Jewish community. And in December, 1955, a stratified national sample was asked by a well-known polling agency whether "any nationality, religious or racial group in this country was a threat to America" and, if so, to name any such group. Only 1 per cent of those questioned answered "Jews," as compared with 20 per cent in 1946 and 5 per cent in 1950.

The equality of status that had earlier been achieved by the Catholic and Jewish religions has now been achieved by the adherents of those religions. The conditions for free and effective competition— that the wares of each competitor have equal access to the market and that no competitor suffer personal discrimination for venturing on the market—have now been satisfied. The third era in American interreligious relationships, the era of creative competition, can truly be said to have begun. The Catholic faith and the Jewish faith no longer have to justify themselves. Catholics and Jews as such are no longer on the defensive. They are now able to devote their efforts to seek to fashion American culture according to their own concepts and values. It is therefore hardly surprising that in recent years Catholic and Jewish groups have been publicly expressing their respective views on public issues, and it is certain that they will continue to do so increasingly.

ARE THERE PROTESTANT, CATHOLIC, AND JEWISH POSITIONS?

To speak of a Protestant position or a Catholic position on a particular public issue is, of course, a generalization (as was the division of interreligious relations into three periods in the preceding section). Social scientists, particularly academicians, are wary of generalizations, and in the field of interreligious relations there is almost a dread of generalizations. Use of the term "Protestant position" is strenuously contested. In view of the hundreds of Protestant denominations how, it is asked, can there be a single Protestant position on anything? At best, all one can accurately say is that "some Protestants believe" or perhaps "many Protestants maintain." Even among Catholics, it is pointed out, there are those who do not favor an exchange of ambassadors with the Vatican or the use of tax-raised funds for parochial school transportation, just as there are Protestants and Jews who do favor each of these steps. It is probable that a majority of married American Catholics practice contraceptive birth control despite the strong position taken by the Church against it. Catholic judges in civil courts freely grant divorces to Catholic litigants, notwithstanding papal condemnation of such action. Recently, a jury in heavily Catholic Providence, Rhode Island, voted to allow a Jewish couple to adopt a child born to Catholic parents, despite the vigorous opposition of the Church to interreligious adoptions.

These and many other instances are cited by social scientists to illustrate how misleading and dangerous generalization may be. Yet, the refusal to generalize, at least in the subject treated in this book, may be even more misleading and more dangerous. In the imperfect and practical world we live in, conduct, and certainly communal conduct, is based upon generalizations. Even if there were no Catholic position or Jewish position on many issues of public importance, the fact remains that most legislators and other public officials believe there are such positions and shape their official conduct accordingly. Many of them frankly admit that their votes or other official conduct in particular cases is based upon such belief. Newspapers frequently report that the defeat of a particular measure resulted from "Catholic opposition."

Actually, there *is* a Catholic position and a Protestant position and a Jewish position on the issues discussed in this book. That there are dissenters in each group as to every one of the issues does not negate the validity of the generalization. Its validity is most apparent in respect to the Catholic position. One who reads the Catholic press cannot fail to observe the almost monolithic uniformity of views on public issues. Modest variations in degree, to be sure, can be discerned. For example, the *Tablet*, organ of the Roman Catholic Archdiocese of Brooklyn, has always been a stanch supporter of Senator Joseph R. McCarthy; the *Pilot*, organ of the Boston Archdiocese, and *America*, the Jesuit weekly, stanch opponents. But the differences between them concerned McCarthy as an individual; there was no fundamental difference between them in their adherence to the strong anti-Communist policy of McCarthy. One cannot find in the official Catholic press any opposition to an exchange of ambassadors with the Vatican or the use of tax-raised funds to aid parochial schools, nor any support for the liberalization of divorce or censorship laws or for diplomatic recognition of Communist China or for the repeal or liberalization of the various internal security laws. The only substantial dissent within articulated Catholicism can be found in the pages of *Commonweal*, a lay publication, highly respected but with little practical influence, and the *Catholic Worker*, a radical publication of extreme views and also with little influence.

The clarity and uniformity of Catholic opinion on issues of public importance resulted from the great and rapid growth in the power and influence of the Catholic Church which in turn led to a polarization of articulated Catholic opinion. It is a generalization but a valid one to say that the Catholic position on a particular issue within the realm of concern of the Catholic Church is the position of the Catholic Church. The polarization of Catholic opinion on these issues led to, or was concomitant with, the counter-polarization of Protestant and Jewish opinion on these issues. (The unification of much of Protestantism in the National Council of Churches was at least partly motivated by considerations of defense against the rising tide of Catholicism.) In other instances, Protestant positions and Jewish positions were self-initiated and evolved independently of a Catholic position; neither Protestant support for Sabbath laws and anti-gambling laws nor Jewish support for American governmental friendliness to Israel can be attributed to the felt need for defense against competitive Catholicism.

Also, lacking the overarching structure of an all-encompassing church, Protestant and Jewish positions are naturally less monolithic. Dissent is likely to be more articulate and better organized; one does not find within Catholicism the equivalent of the bitterly anti-Zionist American Council for Judaism. Nevertheless, on most of the issues considered in this book it is as correct to speak of Protestant and Jewish positions as it is to speak of a Catholic position. The practical unanimity of American Catholicism against the decision of the United States Supreme Court in the McCollum case [1] and its strict interpretation of the principle of separation of church and state is matched by the practical unanimity of American Judaism in support of that decision and its strict interpretation, and by the unanimity of American Protestantism against governmental aid to parochial schools or an ambassador to the Vatican or legislation permitting bingo and lotteries. On some issues, such as the meaning of separation of church and state and the place of religion in public education, Protestant opinion is more divided than either Catholic or Jewish, but even there sufficient agreement can be found among a substantial majority of Protestant groups to justify speaking of a Protestant position or at most two Protestant positions.

[1] Discussed more fully below, pp. 67 ff.

IS COMPETITION GOOD OR BAD?

Is the competition among the major religious faiths desirable or undesirable? Would it be better if the churches limited their efforts to matters of spirit and to preparing their congregants for the kingdom that is not of this earth, rather than seek to shape the culture of the community through intervention in public affairs? A fuller discussion of this question must await the last chapter of this book, since a fair evaluation must in large part be based on how competition actually operates on the American scene and what its consequences are. One preliminary observation, however, is appropriate here.

Cultural competition is consistent with the American spirit and the American tradition. The free enterprise economic system is predicated on the assumption that the greatest temporal good to the greatest number is most likely to be achieved if individual entrepreneurs are free to compete on the open market for public patronage. Anti-monopoly and fair trade laws have been adopted to assure freedom of competition in the economic market. More closely in point, the American political system is predicated on the same assumption. The nation prides itself on its competitive two-party system and condemns the monopolistic one-party system that prevails in totalitarian states. The Constitution guarantees freedom of speech and of the press, a guaranty that the Supreme Court has often said is based on the commitment of the republic to a free trade in ideas. The theory of the Constitution, Justice Oliver Wendell Holmes said in one of his opinions, is that "the best test of truth is the power of the thought to get itself accepted in the competition of the free market." "It is," he continued, "an experiment, as all life is an experiment, [but] that experiment is part of our system."

Moreover, Americans are committed to the experiment not only in material and political wares, but in spiritual wares as well. The guaranty of the free exercise of religion in the Bill of Rights has been interpreted by the Supreme Court to assure freedom of missionary competition among the religious faiths. The Constitution guarantees to unpopular and minority religious faiths equal access to the market of souls enjoyed by the conventional faiths. The Supreme Court has ruled that a street missionary in New York City could not be barred from engaging in his activities even though in the course thereof he attacked other religions, calling Catholicism "a religion of the devil," the Pope an "Antichrist," and Jews "Christ killers." The Court has gone even further and held that non-religion or anti-religion is entitled to compete on equal terms with religion. It therefore refused to permit the State of New York to ban the motion picture *The Miracle* even though it was found by the New York courts to be sacrilegious and to make mockery of religious beliefs.

Competition among religious cultures, moreover, is consistent with the concept of cultural pluralism. True enough, Americans have not always recognized cultural pluralism as a desirable characteristic of their society. On the contrary, not many years ago they were committed to a directly opposite goal—cultural homogeneity. In the period immediately following World War I there were enacted a variety of Federal and State laws seeking to eliminate all cultural differences and mold a single "American type." In the states, laws were enacted with a view of forbidding or discouraging the learning of foreign languages. In Congress an immigration law was passed that severely restricted immigration from lands whose cultures differed from ours, such as those in eastern and southern Europe and in Asia.

Fortunately the more enlightened segment of the community has graduated from this stage of adolescent nationalism. It now not only accepts differences but welcomes them, subscribing to Jefferson's view that uniformity of opinion is no more desirable than uniformity of face and stature. While the national origins quota system, whose avowed purpose was to maintain the "American type" uncontaminated by alien influences, is still part of the immigration laws, more and more political leaders, beginning with former President Harry S. Truman, have denounced it as the offspring of bigotry, and its days are numbered.

However, even if the elimination of the national origins quota system should come within a short time, the nation still will not be able to count on immigration to furnish it with the material for a pluralistic culture. The reason for this is that immigration generally and from all sources has ceased to be a significant element in the make-up of the country's population and culture. Today the whole number of immigrants is exceedingly small, making up but a negligible trickle. It is for this reason that competition among the religious cultures becomes exceedingly important. For the pluralism that was once sustained by the large-scale immigration of diverse ethnic groups must now be nourished from the competitive creativity of the diverse religious groups that make up the American community.

WHAT IS AMERICAN ABOUT THE EXPERIMENT?

Is competition among religious cultures an experiment, and if so what makes it an American experiment? Have not religious groups always sought to dominate and shape the culture of the community of which they were part? Is not what I have called creative competition among religious cultures merely another term for the command of Jesus to his disciples to teach all nations, or for missionary activity by any religious group? Nevertheless, creative competition as it is understood in this book is an experiment, and singularly an American one, and for the following reasons.

In the first place, it is uniquely American to recognize the desirability of religious diversity. Whatever may have been the situation before the rise of Jewish monotheism or outside the Christian world, it remains true that within the orbit of Christian influence religious diversity had uniformly been deemed an evil at the time our republic was established. Indeed, what form of Christianity a state embraced was judged secondary in importance to its embracing a single religion; the Peace of Augsburg in 1555 provided that the religion of any German province should automatically be the religion espoused by the particular prince ruling it at the time. In 1784 James Madison cried out that "torrents of blood have been spilt in the world in vain attempts of the secular arm to extinguish religious discord by proscribing all differences in religious opinion." A century later, Chancellor Bismarck, though avoiding bloodshed, engaged in a *kulturkampf* for the same end of achieving religious uniformity. On the other hand, the mandate of the First Amendment to the American Constitution that "Congress shall make no law respecting an establishment of religion or prohibiting the free exercise thereof" implicitly acknowledged the indispensability of religious diversity in a democratic society. It accorded constitutional sanction to Madison's wise dictum that "security for civil rights must be the same as that for religious rights; it consists in the one case in a multiplicity of interests and in the other in a multiplicity of sects."

In the second place, in America the competition is peaceful. We have been singularly free of the torrents of blood that Madison cried out against. Half the wars of Europe, James Bryce said in *The American Commonwealth*, have arisen from religious differences, but this "whole chapter of debate and strife has remained virtually unopened in the United States." During the first half of the nineteenth century some blood was shed in anti-Catholic riots in Philadelphia, but this was an isolated incident and does not negate the overall peaceful nature of religious competition in America. Of course, as we will see, interreligious differences do lead to interreligious friction and tensions. Undoubtedly, bitterness and acrimony often accompany the competition among American religious groups, but with the one exception already noted the competition has been kept peaceful and unbloody.

In the third place, the competition is free and uncoerced. The state keeps its hands off. It does not exert pressure or influence in favor of one religion or against another, or indeed in favor of religion as against non-religion.

Fourth, and in large measure because of this, there is no formal intervention by religious groups in politics. There is in America no Catholic party or Christian Center party or any political party affiliated with or representing a particular religious sect.

Fifth, and again because of this, the objective of competition is not to capture the state but to convince the community. The religious groups wish to translate their values into communal values mainly through the operation of law. But they seek to achieve this neither by commanding the state (as in theocracies) nor by partnership with it (as in nations where church and state are united). They seek to achieve it by convincing the masters of the state in a democracy—the people—that the values they urge are the best for the community and should be adopted by the political representatives of the community. This they do by taking and defending positions on important public issues affecting the community. An examination of these positions is what this book is about.

2. THE COMPETITORS AND THEIR WARES

PREJUDICE OR POWER?

Social scientists have long been concerned with the conflicts and tensions incident to interracial relations in the United States, particularly, though not exclusively, Negro-white relations. Books, articles, university courses, and teachers' workshops on interracial relations are legion. A whole new field called intercultural education has been developed to deal with the adjustment between racial minorities and the majority culture in which they live. A two-volume classic, Gunnar Myrdal's *An American Dilemma*, has examined every facet of Negro-white relations in the United States.

Sociologists and educators are only beginning to recognize the existence of a problem area in the field of interreligious relations. Some of them are becoming aware that the problems of interreligious relations are likely to be with us for many years after interracial problems will have achieved a reasonably satisfactory solution. The decision of the Supreme Court outlawing racial segregation in the public schools and other publicly owned facilities will ultimately result in the complete adjustment and equality of the Negro in our community, no matter how violent and tense may be the period of transition before that goal is reached. The closing of the wellsprings of immigration will, if it has not already done so, eliminate ethnic differences as a serious intergroup problem area. Religious differences, however, are likely to become more intense and more troublesome before an acceptable solution is reached.

The awareness that interreligious relations comprise a problem area as do interracial relations has caused many social scientists and

19.

group relations workers to treat them as identical, or at least subject to the same evaluations and diagnostic approaches and amenable to the same therapeutic techniques. Just as Negro-white tensions are by their very nature an evil that should be eliminated as quickly as possible, so too Catholic-Protestant or Christian-Jewish tensions are completely evil and should be eradicated. Just as Negro-white tensions are based on prejudice and bigotry, so too are interreligious tensions. Just as the interracial problem will be solved when the Negro is finally and fully accepted as an equal member of the community, so too will the interreligious problem be solved when the Catholic and the Jew are finally and fully accepted as equal members of the community. And just as the elimination of racial prejudice and the solution of the Negro-white problem can be achieved by educating the white majority to the evils of prejudice and to the scientific truths about differences in skin color, so, too, these group relations workers argue, can the solution of the interreligious problem be best achieved by educating the Protestant majority to the evils of religious bigotry and to the religious truth that we are all children of the same God and that differences in the way we worship Him are no more significant than differences in the colors of our skins.

The religious groups themselves frequently take the same approach. When, in 1949, Mrs. Eleanor Roosevelt expressed her opposition to the inclusion of private and parochial schools in any program of Federal aid to education, Cardinal Spellman of New York accused her of anti-Catholic prejudice. The Catholic press consistently charges the organization Protestants and Other Americans United for Separation of Church and State with being the twentieth-century successors of the Know-Nothing and Nativist groups of the nineteenth century. Jews often find anti-Semitic motivations in Christian opposition to Zionist aims or in Catholic efforts to intensify the Christological content of public school Christmas programs.

The history of interreligious relations in America briefly sketched in the previous chapter lends a certain plausibility to such charges. Undoubtedly the most prominent aspect of interreligious relations in the nineteenth and early twentieth centuries was bigotry. It was, however, not basically religious bigotry, but ethnic bigotry. The prejudice and discrimination suffered by the Catholic resulted not primarily from the fact that he was a Catholic, but that he was an

Irish Catholic or an Italian Catholic or a Polish Catholic. Anti-Semitism in America was not aimed at the Jewish religion, but at the Jewish immigrants from Russia and Poland. It is quite probable that if every Catholic and Jewish immigrant who came to this country after our republic was established had been a native Englishman, neither anti-Catholicism nor anti-Semitism would ever have been a serious problem in the United States. For example, the German Catholics who accompanied their Lutheran co-immigrants from Germany and Scandinavia to the Middle West were largely spared this prejudice and were accorded substantially equal treatment.

The truth of the matter is that interracial and interreligious relations are completely dissimilar phenomena, and any intelligent effort to meet the respective problems growing out of them must recognize their basic dissimilarity. Negro-white conflict situations arise wholly out of the fact of skin color differences. Once it is universally accepted that differences in skin color are as meaningless and irrelevant as differences in hair or eye color, and once the effects upon the Negroes of centuries of submerged status disappear, there will no longer be Negro-white conflicts nor Negro-white problems nor, indeed, Negro-white relations. The solution of the Negro-white problem lies in the achievement by the Negro of full and equal status in American society. There is no Negro culture struggling for domination or even for survival; the so-called Negro culture typified by spirituals, *Porgy and Bess*, and jazz is a pseudo-Negro culture imposed by the dominant white majority and no more authentically Negro than *Show Boat* and minstrels. Since there is no "Negroism," anti-Negroism is simply "anti-Negroes." Since there is, on the other hand, a real Catholicism and a real Judaism each with a mission and adherents committed to its survival and extension, anti-Catholicism (or, more accurately, pro-Protestantism or pro-secularism) and anti-Judaism (or, more accurately, pro-Christianism) are not the same as "anti-Catholics" and "anti-Jews," and attempts to treat them as the same are both unfair and ineffectual.

A number of social scientists, recognizing the basic difference between interreligious and interracial relations, have adopted another approach. They see interreligious relations and conflicts largely in terms of Catholic-non-Catholic relations and conflicts. They recognize that Protestant-Jewish relations have areas of tension and that conflict and disagreement exist within Protestantism and within Judaism. But these are comparatively minor areas of tension; the major area is the Catholic-non-Catholic conflict. Moreover, these social scientists see the problem almost exclusively against the background of the Catholic Church. It is not, to them, a problem of Catholics in a community that includes Protestants and Jews; nor of Catholicism in a society that encompasses Protestantism and Judaism. To them the problem is primarily the adjustment of the Catholic Church to American democracy and American democracy to the Catholic Church. Finally, they see the conflict as simply a struggle for power. The motivating force behind the efforts of the Church in the arena of public issues is first to maintain its power over its own communicants and secondly to extend that power over the entire American community. It need hardly be said that many Protestants and not a few Jews agree with this analysis.

It is true that Catholic-non-Catholic relations constitute the major area of interreligious tension and conflict today. It is also true that because of the nature of Catholicism, the Catholic community, and the Catholic Church, the pivot on which Catholic-non-Catholic relations turn is the Catholic Church. However, it is as inaccurate and unjust to ascribe to the naked desire for power the efforts of the Church in the field of public issues as it is to ascribe to prejudice and bigotry the efforts of non-Catholics in defending and promoting positions opposed to those of the Church. To deem the activities of the Catholic Church in the arena of public issues as exclusively or even primarily the manifestations of an institutional struggle for power is to close one's eyes to the basic underlying motivations. Desire for power is a simple answer to the question troubling so many non-Catholics: Why does the Church act that way? But like all simple answers to complex problems, it is an inaccurate and certainly an inadequate answer.

To be sure, there are within the Catholic Church seekers after power for its own sake, a circumstance to be expected in an institution as vast as the Church with so many thousands of bishops and priests. Yet if all that were involved were a struggle to obtain and maintain power, the Church could not possibly have survived two thousand years and exert the tremendous influence over so many millions of persons that it does today. History has shown that institutions whose sole or principal goal is power have remarkably short life expectancies.

The Catholic Church, I submit, does not take the positions it does on public issues and pursue the activities it does in support of those positions in order to gain power. It does not seek to shape America's cultural patterns in order to control America. The reverse is far closer to the truth. It seeks power in order to shape America's culture. Power is the means, not the end. The Catholic Church acts the way it does because it is profoundly and irrevocably committed to a philosophy of life and a way of living that is rather new and strange and undoubtedly frightening to an America that, through a paradoxical but apparently workable alliance of Protestantism and secular humanism, believes it has achieved the best of all possible worlds this side of Eden. And the counteractions of American Protestantism are not motivated simply by a desire to retain power or to ward off a rival's struggle for power, but by a deeply felt need to defend a philosophy of life and a way of living threatened by what appears to many Protestants to be the rising tide of Catholicism. As will be seen throughout the book, the reason that American Judaism is generally more sympathetic to the Protestant position than to the Catholic is that the Jewish way of life in America is more in harmony with that of American Protestantism than of American Catholicism. The cultural alliance between American liberal Protestantism and secular humanism is eminently satisfactory to the Jewish community; it is not satisfactory to the Catholic Church.

An understanding of the competition among these religious groups in the arena of public issues, therefore, requires an understanding of their differing philosophies and ways of life. This in turn requires a comprehension of at least their basic doctrines. Although differences in creeds and dogma are no longer as significant in interreligious relationships as they were in colonial times, they nevertheless underlie all interreligious relations.

For example, consider the position of the Catholic Church on interreligious adoptions. As we will see in a later chapter, the Church vigorously supports laws and would make it impossible for a couple of one faith to adopt a child born to a mother of different faith. This position can be explained in terms of either power or dogma. The former explanation would be based on the fact that probably most cases of interreligious adoptions involve the adoption by a non-Catholic couple of a child born to a Catholic mother, and that prohibition of such adoptions would eliminate a possible weakening of Catholic power, which is based upon the proportion of Catholics to the whole population. On the other hand, the same position may be explained by the Catholic dogma of the immutability of baptism, the dogma of "once a Catholic always a Catholic."

But the Catholic Church also takes positions that are completely meaningless or self-defeating if considered exclusively in terms of a power struggle and without regard to creed and dogma. The Church strongly supports legislation forbidding the dissemination of information concerning contraceptive birth control even to married couples. Since contraceptive birth control is not considered sinful by the other major faiths, the absence of secular legislation binding equally on Catholics and non-Catholics would seem to be to the advantage of the Catholic Church, for it would result (as it actually does since such laws are rarely enforced even where they are still on the books) in larger Catholic than non-Catholic families. The Catholic position on birth control laws makes sense only in the light of Catholic dogma that contraception is a violation of natural law and is immoral even when practiced by non-Catholics.

What is true of the Catholic Church is likewise true of Protestantism and Judaism, although perhaps not quite as obviously. The organizational spokesmen of these faiths also take positions on public issues whose real explanation is to be found in their philosophies, dogmas, and creeds rather than in terms of a struggle for power.

This does not mean that the considerations of power and church status play no role in determining the positions that each faith takes on public issues. Nor does it mean that practical considerations are disregarded or that the exigencies of American public opinion do not on occasion dictate what appears to be a compromise with principle and dogma. Dogmatically, the Catholic Church deems the separation of church and state to be wrong. The practical realization of America's commitment to that principle requires the spokesmen for the Church to refrain from a direct attack on the principle and indeed often to express adherence to it. Similarly, there is nothing in the dogmas or traditions of Judaism that supports a separation of sacred from secular powers. No such separation can be found in the Torah of Moses or in the Talmud. Nevertheless, the American rabbinate is as committed to the principle of separation of church and state as the most secularist libertarian, at least in part because it realizes that as a minority faith Judaism is most secure if church and state are kept apart. And lest it be assumed that Protestantism never compromises principle for practical considerations, let it be noted that the opposition of Protestantism to financial governmental aid to religion and religious education, on the grounds that such aid violates the principle of the separation of church and state, is not reflected in any similar opposition to the grant to churches of exemption from property taxes.

There are thus instances where commitment to creed and principle impels the religious groups to take positions disadvantageous from the viewpoint of practical power politics. There are also instances where practical considerations compel the religious groups to take positions not wholly consistent with creed and principle. It must, however, be understood that both types of instances are exceptional rather than usual. It will become manifest throughout this book that in the overwhelming majority of cases the position a religious group takes on an issue of public importance is consistent with its philosophy and dogma and at the same time consistent with considerations of institutional power and status. It is for that reason that at least a summary examination is required of the principal elements of creed and dogma of each of the faiths most proximately related to their positions on public issues, as well as of the nature and character of their institutional structures. To that examination the remainder of this chapter is devoted.

NEW ENGLAND CALVINISM

American religious culture originated in Calvinist New England. Even today the nation's moral standards and criminal codes largely reflect the Puritan values of seventeenth and eighteenth century Calvinism. Some of the major aspects of Calvinist dogma and church structure relevant to our consideration of competition among religious cultures in the market place of public issues are the following:

1. *The wickedness of man.* Orthodox Calvinism was obsessed with the dogma of original sin. Men were inherently evil and, with the exception of a few whom God selected to save, were doomed to damnation. This obsession with the inherent fallibility of all men did imply a concept of egalitarianism which was an important part of New England's heritage to American democracy.

2. *Compulsion and election.* It follows from this that the idea that men should be free in matters of faith and morals was alien and repugnant to New England Calvinism. If man were free to choose, he would invariably choose error and evil. Election belongs exclusively

to God; the obligation of man is to obey the word of God as communicated through the church. It is well known that the Puritans came to America not to establish religious liberty but to secure freedom of worship for themselves alone. They had no hesitation in imposing upon articulate dissenters the same persecution that they had suffered at the hands of the Anglican Church.

3. *Church and state.* For the same reasons, the concept of separation of church and state was alien and repugnant to New England Calvinism. The Congregationalist Church of Massachusetts was the last of all American churches to become disestablished, and when separation was finally achieved in 1833 it was against the desires of the church.

4. *Man's purpose in life.* Man's sole purpose in life was the glorification of God. Whatever detracted from man's efforts and activities in the pursuit of this end was necessarily evil. Happiness, as the term is generally understood, if not intrinsically evil was certainly not the aim of life.

5. *Austerity and simplicity.* The Puritan mind abhorred pomp, pageantry, and ornateness. Puritan church services centered on the sermon and eschewed all rites and ritual.

6. *The moral standards.* Puritan moral standards were the strictest of all among the tributaries to American culture. The principal evils were lewdness, covetousness, anger, untruthfulness, Sabbath-breaking, vanity, gossiping, and idleness.

ANGLICANISM

As Congregational Calvinism was the established church in New England, so Anglicanism was the established church in Virginia and the Southern colonies. However, while Calvinism played a tremendous role in shaping American cultural patterns, the contributions of Anglicanism were comparatively insignificant. The religion and culture of Anglicanism after the disappearance of early Calvinist influence, fitted well the needs of the Southern plantation aristocracy (as they had fitted the needs of the Tudor and Stuart aristocracies), and whatever influence Anglicanism might have on American culture vanished along with the disappearance of the plantation aristocracy.

The Protestantism of the South was to become that of the popular denominations, the Baptists, the Methodists, and other dissenting sects. Aristocratic Anglicanism, known after the Revolution as Episcopalianism, had little to offer to the poor white tiller of the soil or the poorer black slave. Besides, the Episcopalians chose the wrong (i.e., losing) side in the Revolution. Most of their clergy were not merely unsympathetic to the Revolution but were ardent and active Loyalists, and with the success of the Revolution, followed quickly by the disestablishment of their church in Virginia, Episcopalianism rapidly lost whatever influence it had previously exerted on Southern cultural patterns and moral standards. The disappearance of Episcopalianism as a culture or moral force in the South, which had been its citadel, is evidenced by the fact that the South has long been the stronghold of the Prohibitionist movement although Episcopalianism is among the minority of Protestant denominations which does not frown upon the consumption of intoxicating liquors.

PROTESTANT DISSENT

Protestant dissent, as the term is used here, includes about all of American Protestantism outside established Congregationalism in New England and established Anglicanism in the South. It thus comprises such divergent sects as the Unitarians and Universalists in New England, the Quakers, Presbyterians, and Moravians in the middle colonies, the Baptists in the South and the Methodists in the West. Despite this divergence, there is in Protestant dissent a substantial common core of philosophy and belief which has had a great influence in shaping American culture, and particularly American political culture. As much as any other force in American history, Protestant dissent has been responsible for the libertarian democracy that characterizes American political society.

Protestant dissent antedated the Great Awakening of the mid-eighteenth century, but it received a strong impetus from that evangelical revival which originated in New England and spread throughout the colonies. It succeeded because its beliefs and way of living were admirably suited (or became suited) to a society living on an expanding frontier. Neither the closely knit church-Calvinism of New England nor the aristocratic Anglicanism of Virginia could live, much less flourish, in the sparsely settled Indian country. A pioneer traveling by mule or wagon to establish a home in a log cabin miles away from any other person could take with him only such religion as could be encompassed in a small Bible and could be expressed through the reading of that Bible and through individual, personal communion with God. There was no place on the frontier for imposing church edifices, erudite theology, or an ecclesiastical hierarchy. Since by necessity every man was a priest and expounder of faith to his congregation (i.e., his family), the faith must needs be simple, individualistic, and personal. Hence, Protestant dissent was founded on a Bible that was not only all-sufficient but was and had to be self-explanatory and equally understandable to all who could read. This, too, explains the sanctity of individual conscience in Protestant dissent—a concept completely unacceptable in the Roman Catholic ethic and hardly more welcome in established Calvinism or established Anglicanism.

By recognizing that Protestant dissent was the creature of the expanding frontier, we can appreciate the great contribution it made to the evolution of American culture and its relevance to our consideration of the positions taken by the religious groups on public issues. Besides being individual rather than church-centered, nonclerical if not anti-clerical, personal rather than creedal, it was completely democratic and egalitarian. It accepted the Calvinist moral code and Calvinist austerity and simplicity, but it was far less pessimistic than Calvinism and far more secularistic or this-worldly. Perhaps more important, unlike Calvinism, Anglicanism, and Roman Catholicism, it was committed to voluntarism in faith. It rebelled against coercion in matters of conscience and considered religion a matter of election rather than of status. Strictly speaking, religion related only to adults, since only adults could make a choice, and to this day, unlike Catholicism and Judaism, Protestantism considers only adults in estimating its membership.

Because of its commitment to voluntarism in matters of conscience, Protestant dissent was steadfastly opposed to any union of church and state. It was, as we shall see in the next chapter, an alliance between Protestant dissent and the secular humanism of European deism and rationalism that was responsible for launching the American experiment of the separation of church and state. The same alliance was also responsible for America's libertarian tradition in political affairs and for the great freedoms secured in our Bill of Rights.

SECULAR HUMANISM [1]

Only in a broad sense can the wave of deism that swept America in the last quarter of the eighteenth century be called a religious movement. If the term "religion" is viewed as connoting organized religion, then eighteenth-century deism was non-religious if not actually anti-religious. Originating in England, it became united in America with the humanistic rationalism of the French Enlightenment. This union was perhaps the most potent cultural and intellectual force when the American republic was established.

William Warren Sweet, in his *Religion in the Development of American Culture,* has acutely noted that "the United States of America began as a free and independent nation with organized religion at a low ebb." Next to the Bible, the most widely read and widely discussed book was Tom Paine's scoffing attack on the Bible, *The Age of Reason.* Religious skepticism permeated the universities. Lyman Beecher described the period as "the day of the infidelity of the Tom Paine school" when most of his students at Yale "were infidels and called each other Voltaire, Rousseau, d'Alembert. . . ." Probably not more than 10 per cent of the population was affiliated with any church. (Today well over half the population avow membership in some religious group.) None of the first seven Presidents of the United States was formally affiliated with any church. The drafters of the Constitution of the United States studiously avoided all reference to God in their document. The treaty negotiated with Tripoli in 1797 squarely avowed that "the government of the United States of America is not, in any sense, founded on the Christian religion." Unless the word "religious" is given an extremely broad or irrelevant meaning, the frequently heard statement that the framers of our Constitution and the founders of the republic were religious is closer to myth than to history.

Perhaps it was a historical accident that the American republic was founded during the period when organized religion was at its lowest ebb. If the Constitution had been written a quarter of a century earlier at the time of the established churches and widespread religiosity, America might have had a different type of government and a different type of relationship between church and state. What

[1] The term "secular humanism" is used in this book not to mean a consciously non-theistic movement, but merely the influence of those unaffiliated with organized religion and concerned with human values.

is certain, however, is that the deistic rationalism of late eighteenth century America (more often referred to in this book by the more modern term, secular humanism) has had a tremendous influence in American history. Out of its alliance with Protestant dissent evolved the major patterns of American political, social, and intellectual (though not moral) culture.

For our purposes, probably the most important aspect of deism was its rejection of the concept of original sin and its romantic counterassumption of the inherent goodness of man. It is not too much to say that our constitutional liberties are predicated on this optimistic assumption, for they proceed on the premise that given freedom —of belief, of thought, of speech, of association—men can be counted on to do the right thing. From that assumption too flowed the other aspects of deistic rationalism: its anti-authoritarianism in church and in state (it was the French-influenced anti-Federalists who were most opposed to and suspicious of a strong national government); its anti-clericalism; its secularism (i.e., emphasis on this world); its egalitarianism ("All men are created equal," said the deist Jefferson in the Declaration of Independence); its faith in reason; its opposition to coercion in matters of conscience and belief; its commitment to voluntarism; its libertarianism; its agreement with Protestant dissent that religion is a matter of free election rather than of inherited or imposed status. "No man," said John Locke, whose influence on American thought was immeasurable, "by nature is bound unto any particular church or sect, but everyone joins himself voluntarily to that society in which he believes he has found that profession and worship which is truly acceptable to God. A church is a society of members voluntarily uniting to that end."

Perhaps the best evidence of the influence of deism on American ideals is the fact that the two basic documents of American freedom, the Declaration of Independence (notwithstanding its numerous references to God and Providence) and the Bill of Rights breathe its spirit.

ROMAN CATHOLICISM

The domination of our moral culture by the alliance of Calvinism and Protestant dissent, and the domination of our political and social culture by the alliance of Protestant dissent and secular humanism now face their most serious challenge. It is a challenge from a source whose confidence in itself and in its ability to fashion the future of America closer to its own desires seems to be justified ever increasingly by the daily events of American life and far more than anyone could have dreamed a bare three decades ago.

Before the present generation, Roman Catholicism in America was on the defensive. Even in that capacity it was able indirectly and sporadically to effect some changes in American cultural patterns. This it did partly through the determination and commitment of its adherents, but more importantly through alliances with other forces. Through an alliance with secular humanism it was able, as we shall see in a later chapter, to secularize our public educational system. Through an alliance with Jewish radicalism it was able to educate a major part of American labor—traditionally individualistic and independent—to accept the collective discipline of unionism. But its successful efforts to secularize the public schools were purely defensive in motivation, undertaken by the need to protect its children from Protestant teachings and Protestant proselytization. And its influence in the growth of the labor union movement was largely unintended and indirect; it resulted simply from the fact that the discipline that Catholic workers learned in their churches could practically be transferred to their union halls. It is only in recent years that Roman Catholicism has become sufficiently strong to take a positive or aggressive role in shaping American culture either substantially alone (e.g., as in framing divorce and family laws) or in alliances in which it is the dominant partner (e.g., as in the campaign to return religion to the public schools).

Today, barely past mid-century, the influence of Catholicism has reached a point in most states and in the Federal government where, while it cannot obtain the enactment of every measure it supports (e.g., Federal aid to parochial schools, or an ambassador to the Vatican), it can defeat the enactment of any measure that it vigorously opposes (e.g., Federal aid to education that excludes parochial schools, or divorce reform). Indeed, within the past few years it has been able almost singlehandedly to obtain the enactment of some Federal measures, such as the adoption of "In God We Trust" as the official national motto, or the inclusion of "under God" in the Pledge of Allegiance to the flag. These, it is true, affect our culture only slightly and peripherally and, for whatever reason, evoked practically no manifest opposition. Yet they are surely a harbinger of more significant things to come. The future of American culture will have to reckon with Roman Catholicism.

There are a variety of reasons for what appears to be an emerging dominance of Catholicism in American life. One of them undoubtedly is the nature of its institutional structure—strongly centralized, monolithic, purposeful, possessed of powerful spiritual sanctions over its communicants. In America—not necessarily elsewhere to the same extent—Catholicism and the Catholic Church are for all practical purposes identical. (The same cannot be said of Protestantism or Judaism.) Another reason is undoubtedly that Catholicism offers a spiritual certainty and emotional security in an age beset by fear of thermonuclear extermination. The vigor of Catholic opposition to communism may be a third. But whatever the reason, the role of Catholicism as a major cultural competitor requires a recognition of the most important of its creeds and beliefs that are relevant to its positions on public issues.

1. *Salvation and damnation.* Far more than Protestantism or Judaism, Catholicism is concerned with the future world. One has to go back to seventeenth-century Calvinism to find a religion in which salvation or damnation after death is of such importance before death. Whereas in Calvinism nothing man does in this life can affect his fate in the future life, in Catholicism almost nothing man does in this life can fail to affect it. Unless one understands the centrality of salvation or damnation after death in Catholicism one cannot understand, much less appreciate or sympathize with, the intensity of its opposition to secularism (i.e., this-worldism), or its position on such issues as birth control, abortion, and divorce, among others.

2. *Outside the Church there is no salvation.* The exact meaning of this dogma is not entirely clear even within Catholicism; Catholic theologians themselves disagree. While all agree that some persons who have never undergone the rite of Catholic baptism may nevertheless be saved, there is no agreement as to exactly which non-Catholics qualify. But there is unanimous agreement that at the very minimum the surest way to salvation is through the Catholic Church. Without an understanding of this dogma it is impossible to understand the Catholic position on such issues as, for example, interreligious adoptions.

3. *No exit, or the immutability of baptism.* It is also impossible to understand the Catholic position on interreligious adoptions and other issues without appreciation of the dogma that, as a practical

matter, a person who undergoes valid Catholic baptism acquires the Catholic religion for life and nothing he may do can change that status.

4. *Religion a status, not an election.* Catholic doctrine deems religion not something one elects (although, of course, one may elect it) but a status acquired at and by birth. According to practical Catholic doctrine a child born to a Catholic mother is a Catholic and remains such for life even if not baptized. For such a child baptism is relevant only to salvation and not, as in the case of children born to non-Catholic mothers, also to acquisition of the Catholic religion.

5. *The one true Church.* Catholics believe—and at the pain of mortal sin must believe—that Jesus established but one faith, the Catholic faith, and one church, the Catholic Church. All other so-called religions are either schismatic, heretical, or pagan, and therefore false or erroneous. Moreover, a Catholic must avoid any conduct that might imply the equality of religions. It is this dogma that explains the refusal of Catholic priests to join ministerial associations and underlies the suspicious if not antipathetic attitude of the Church to the National Conference of Christians and Jews and other interfaith movements, as well as its refusal to join the Protestants and the Eastern Orthodox churches in any ecumenical endeavor or organization, such as the National Council of Churches.

6. *The centrality of the Church.* It is the aim of Catholicism, particularly American Catholicism, to make the Church the center of the life and activities of Catholics. This results in what is called Catholic separatism. It is manifested by the plethora of Catholic organizations, such as Catholic lawyers' guilds, Catholic War Veterans, Catholic teachers' associations, Catholic policemen and firemen's associations, and even Catholic trade unions, each with a priest or priests not merely to advise but, if necessary, to control. (Parenthetically it should be noted that a similar separatism, if perhaps not so thoroughgoing, may be found in American Judaism. However, in Judaism the separatism, until recently, was not voluntary but imposed by Christian anti-Semitism, and was not synagogue-centered. At the present time there does appear to be a growing voluntary separatism in Judaism, and it seems to be becoming synagogue-centered. This development is in some measure attributable to the flight to the suburbs and to the influence of the Catholic model.)

7. *Emphasis on ritual and externals.* Catholics believe that through

Jesus God made clear to men that He wished to be worshiped in a particular way. Catholic clerics find themselves unable to accept the often-heard statement: "After all, we all worship one God. We differ *only* in the way we worship Him." To them the use of the word "only" constitutes a disparagement of God's expressed will that He be worshiped exclusively according to the rites of the Roman Catholic Church. For that reason Catholicism places a major emphasis on ritual and external manifestations of faith. Ceremonialism and pageantry are prominent features of Catholic ritual. (So too are they of High Episcopalianism, Eastern Orthodoxy and Orthodox Judaism.) Meditation and silent or individual prayer have little place in Catholicism. Formalization of worship, verbalizations, tangible objects such as crosses, statues, rosary beads, holy medals, etc., are all characteristics of Catholic belief. It is this aspect of Catholicism that explains Catholic support for the erection of crosses in public parks or putting "In God We Trust" on our currency and postage stamps.

8. *Original sin and the wickedness of man.* Only in seventeenth-century Calvinism does one find such concern with original sin and the essentially evil nature of man as one finds in Roman Catholicism. Left to his own, runs the assumption, man will always choose evil rather than good. Hence, Catholicism has no sympathy for voluntarism in matters of faith or morals. It emphasizes respect for authority and obedience to superiors. It views the ideal society as one patterned after the hierarchical Roman Church wherein every member owes the obligation of implicit obedience to a superior. Catholicism has little use for the so-called progressive or permissive education. Its schools place great emphasis on discipline and obedience. It frowns on individuality and favors uniformity and conformity. While it has learned to accept democracy in its political world, it sees no place for it in the world of faith and morals.

JUDAISM

Judaism presents the rather remarkable instance of a religion that has adjusted itself happily to the Protestant dissent—secular-humanist culture of America. The Judaism that came to this country from Europe was almost exclusively Orthodox Judaism, which in many respects is similar in its philosophy and way of living to Roman

Catholicism. Like the latter it views religion as a matter of inherited status rather than election and deems a child automatically to acquire at its birth the religion of its mother. Like Roman Catholicism it places great emphasis on ritual and on externals. It, too, is greatly concerned with sin and with the world to come. In America, however, Reform or Liberal Judaism, which originated in Germany, and Conservative Judaism, which arose here, have taken on much of the coloration of Protestant secular humanism.

Even Orthodox Judaism has not remained unaffected. Actually, the present movement of the Jews to suburbs where but one synagogue is practicable, is resulting in a merging of the three branches. The suburban synagogue, called with increasing frequency the "Jewish Center" of the particular community, represents a compromise between Reform worship, which, like Protestant dissent, de-emphasizes ritual and creed, making the sermon and non-formalized (English) prayers and hymns the core of the service, and Orthodox worship wherein ritual and formalized Hebrew prayers are the major elements.

Of all the major religious groups, American Jews are probably the most secularist in the sense of being most concerned with this life and its affairs and problems. They probably have the greatest faith in democracy, not only in political society but in the world of religion and morality. All in all, they are quite happy with the way the American political system and American culture have developed and are no less than the Protestants concerned about the challenge to that culture posed by the rising tide of Roman Catholicism. It is for that reason that the Jewish position on public issues far more often coincides with the Protestant than the Catholic position. This is another reason why interreligious conflicts and tensions in the United States revolve largely around Catholic-non-Catholic relations rather than Christian-Jewish relations.

3. RELIGION AND THE STATE

RELIGIOUS LIBERTY IN CATHOLIC DOGMA, HISTORY, AND PRACTICE

Perhaps nowhere else is the clash between Catholic dogma and libertarianism more dramatically manifested than in the relation of religion to the state, and more specifically in the matter of religious liberty. The dogma of Catholicism is not hospitable to concepts of freedom in matters of faith. A religion that considers itself the only true faith and its rites the only way to salvation is not likely to be sympathetic to the claims of what it deems erroneous and heretical beliefs, nor of the demands of weak if not inherently evil men to espouse those beliefs.

Let it be said at the outset that the creed of Calvinism, of established Anglicanism or, for that matter, of biblical or Talmudic Judaism is hardly more liberal in matters of faith. None of these religions, however, permanently influenced the evolution of American principles of church-state relations, and all of them have long adjusted themselves to those principles. The adjustment of Catholicism is more recent and still not entirely completed. Moreover, as we shall shortly see, Protestantism and Judaism are, perhaps unfairly, suspicious and somewhat skeptical about the wholeheartedness and permanence of that adjustment—considerably more so than they are about the adjustments made by Calvinism, Anglicanism, and Judaism.

In any event, it is Catholic antipathy to religious liberty that constitutes the most frequent ground of attack upon it by non-Catholics. They find much in Catholic dogmatic literature that expresses this hostility. Frequently cited by non-Catholic critics is the editorial appearing in the April, 1945, issue of *Civilta Cattolica*, organ of the Jesuit order in Rome:

The Roman Catholic Church, convinced through its divine prerogatives of being the only true Church, must demand the right of freedom for herself alone, because such a right can only be possessed by truth, never by error. As to other religions, the Church will certainly never draw the sword, but she will require that by legitimate means they shall not be allowed to propagate false doctrine. Consequently, in a state where the majority of people are Catholic, the Church will require that legal existence be denied to error, and that if religious minorities actually exist, they shall have only a de facto *existence, without opportunity to spread their beliefs. . . . In some countries, Catholics will be obliged to ask full religious freedom for all, resigned at being forced to cohabit where they alone should rightfully be allowed to live. But in doing this the Church does not renounce her thesis, which remains the most imperative of her laws, but merely adapts herself to* de facto *conditions, which must be taken into account in practical affairs. . . . The Church cannot blush for her own want of tolerance, as she asserts it in principle and applies it in practice.*

Catholic dogmatic commitment to the exclusiveness of its own truth and to the falsity of other claims to truth would appear logically not only to justify this position but to require it. Thus, say Ryan and Boland in their authoritative *Catholic Principles of Politics*, "the fact that the individual may in good faith think that his false religion is true gives him no more right to propagate it than the sincerity of the alien anarchist entitles him to advocate his abominable political theories in the United States, or than the perverted ethical notions of the dealer in obscene literature confer upon him a right to corrupt the morals of the community." Catholic dogma does not recognize any difference between the falsity and evil of anarchism or obscenity and the falsity and evil of non-Catholic religions. Nor does it acknowledge the moral right of a political state to recognize a difference between them or to treat them differently. It is, said Leo XIII, no more lawful for the state than for the individual to disregard differences in religions and hold them all to be equal.[1]

It can hardly be denied that the history of Christianity reveals many instances in which the Roman Catholic Church called upon

[1] See below, p. 51, for the statement by Leo XIII.

the coercive arm of the state to enforce its claim to exclusive possession of religious truth and to suppress other beliefs as error and evil.
It was St. Augustine who justified the persecution of heretics on
the ground that it was more benevolent that heretics should be
purged of their sin than that they should die unsaved, "for what is a
worse killer of the soul than freedom to err?" The long and bloody
history of the Holy Inquisition remains the most tragic manifestation
of Roman Catholic dogma that error has no right to exist.

Fortunately these pages of history have long been turned and are
not likely to be reopened. But, critics of Catholicism charge, even
today the practical consequences of Catholic aversion to freedom in
matters of conscience can be observed. Spain is invariably pointed to
as a case history of the treatment of non-Catholic religions in a nation in the Catholic tradition. While Spanish law states that "none
shall be molested for their religious beliefs or the private practices
of their worship," it also states that "no other ceremonies or external
demonstrations than those of the Catholic religion shall be permitted." Protestants, it is true, are not persecuted by the government; their ministers enjoy freedom of the pulpit, and their children
receive religious education in their Sunday schools, using in their
classrooms Protestant religious books that their parents may freely
print for their own use. In short, Protestants have full freedom of
private religious practice.

But Protestants do not have full freedom to practice their religion
publicly. Their chapels may not display exterior evidence of the
nature of the service conducted within the walls. Protestants may
not publish or import Bibles for general circulation; they may not
open new churches or reopen closed ones without a special permit,
which may be arbitrarily refused. Protestant proselytizing, propa-
gandizing, and even public demonstrations are forbidden. Other than
Sunday schools, Protestants may not conduct religious schools but
must send their children either to Catholic schools or to the public
schools, and even in the latter their children must participate in
Catholic instruction.

THE CATHOLIC REPLY

This, then, is the charge leveled against Catholicism and the Catholic Church. What is the Catholic reply? In substance, the reply of

American Catholics is that while every individual statement made in the indictment is true, the whole is false. It is false because it is not the whole truth. The picture revealed by the whole truth is radically different from that presented by a deliberate selection of some truths.

Consider, for example, the Inquisition and other instances of medieval Catholic persecution of heretics. These are neither denied nor defended by American Catholics. What they object to is the presentation of these instances as an aspect of the history of Catholicism rather than an aspect of the history of civilization. In the Middle Ages, Catholics in power engaged in persecution and oppression not because they were Catholics but because they were persons in power during an era when persons in power normally engaged in persecution and oppression. The proof lies in the conduct of non-Catholics in power. If Catholics persecuted non-Catholics, so did non-Catholics persecute Catholics and different non-Catholics. It was not a Catholic, but Luther, the father of Protestantism, who said that "heretics are not to be disputed with, but to be condemned unheard, and whilst they perish by fire, the faithful ought to pursue the evil to its source and bathe their hands in the blood of the Catholic bishops." Again, it was the Protestant Calvin who said that "whoever shall now contend that it is unjust to put heretics and blasphemers to death, will, knowingly and willingly, incur their very guilt."

In this country, Catholics point out, the persecutors and oppressors have been exclusively Protestant. The Quakers who were put to death in New England were the victims of Protestantism, not Catholicism. The heretics who filled the jails of Virginia in Madison's day were put there by Protestants, not Catholics. In United States history, Catholics point out, Protestants have never been persecuted by Catholics, even in Maryland when it was a Catholic-controlled colony, whereas Catholics have been persecuted by Protestants. The full and true picture does not consist merely of a tale of Catholic persecution but is delineated in the words of the United States Supreme Court in a 1947 decision:

With the power of government supporting them, at various times and places, Catholics had persecuted Protestants, Protestants had persecuted Catholics, Protestant sects had persecuted other Protestant sects, Catholics of one shade of belief had persecuted Catholics of another shade of belief, and all of these had from time to time persecuted Jews.

What is true of earlier persecutions is true of the contemporary scene. Protestants are oppressed and discriminated against in Spain, not because Spain is a Catholic state but because it is a totalitarian state, and it is in the nature of a totalitarian state to oppress and discriminate against minorities. Non-Catholic totalitarian states oppress and discriminate against religious and ethnic minorities no less than do Catholic totalitarian states: witness atheistic Soviet Russia on the one hand or Moslem Saudi Arabia on the other. Conversely, democratic countries in the Catholic tradition grant liberty to religious minorities no less than do non-Catholic states: witness Ireland, for example, whose constitution acknowledges the special position of the Catholic Church and of the Catholic religion, professed by the great majority of the citizens, and yet accords full religious freedom to Protestants, Jews, and other non-Catholics.

The statements on religious error and religious freedom found in Catholic dogma present a different and more difficult problem for Catholic spokesmen. The difficulty lies in their reluctance to give what is probably the most effective answer. These statements are based upon papal pronouncements made during the centuries, and the high estate held by respect for authority in the Catholic scheme of things makes it difficult and embarrassing for Catholics to say what they otherwise would say—that these pronouncements are not to be taken too seriously.

Actually, that is what in effect is said by such leading Catholic thinkers as John Courtney Murray and Heinrich Rommen. And they are not merely saying it to the non-Catholic world, but are arguing it eloquently within Catholicism. The papal pronouncements, they say, must be understood in the context of the time, place, and situation in which they were uttered. They are not to be understood nor were they intended to be understood as abolutes, true for all times and in all circumstances. They were promulgated as defensive measures to protect the Church and Catholicism when they were in danger and under attack. They are not to be taken as either required or desirable even in countries which are overwhelmingly Catholic in their population. As Rommen has said, "the modern Bill of Rights and the inviolability of the sincere conscience must be jealously respected by a Catholic civilization, if ever the dream of a wholly Catholic world is to be realized."

It remains true, however, that what is generally considered as authoritative Catholic thought does not go this far. The papal pro-

nouncements are accepted as correct in principle. The authoritative
organs of the Catholic Church in America, such as the *American
Ecclesiastical Review*, contest the validity of Father Murray's con-
tention that even in a Catholic state freedom to err must be respected. To them, in principle, freedom of worship remains, in the
words of the *Catholic Dictionary*, "the inalienable right of all men
to worship God according to the teaching of the Catholic Church."

The Catholic position is that a sharp distinction must be made
between principle and practice. Ryan and Boland, *Civilta Cattolica*,
the *Catholic Dictionary*, and the papal encyclicals on which these
and similar pronouncements are based are all correct in principle,
but they have no practical significance and no relevance to interreligious relations in the United States. These doctrines are applicable
only to a Catholic state, that is, one in which all or almost all of
the inhabitants are Catholics. Since there is not the slightest chance
that this will happen in America in the foreseeable future, there is
no reason for fear on the part of non-Catholics. Many Catholics believe that Protestants and Jews use the dogmatic statements on religious liberty in Catholic teachings as a stick to beat Catholics with,
and not as an expression of real concern.

Nor do Catholics rest on the defensive. They express particular
grievance at Protestant and Jewish concern about restrictions on
religious liberty in Catholic countries. They contrast this with Protestant and Jewish silence with respect to restrictions on Catholics in
such Protestant countries as Sweden, or the exclusion of Jesuits from
Switzerland, or the infringements on religious liberty in Israel, or,
above all, the persecution of the Catholic Church and its clergymen
in countries under Communist control. The comparative silence of
Protestantism and Judaism when Catholic religious freedom is infringed, they suggest, casts doubt upon the sincerity of Protestant
and Jewish protests against similar infringements in Catholic countries.

THE FAITHS AND FREEDOM

The positions of the three faiths in respect to religious freedom
can be summarized somewhat as follows. American Protestantism
expresses unqualified commitment to full religious freedom. It has
made a complete adjustment to the libertarianism of the alliance of

dissent and humanism. The Calvinist and the Episcopalian denominations (which have by now merged into Protestant dissent) no less than the Baptists and the Quakers assert the right, both in principle and in practice, to differ in matters of faith, to worship freely, and to propagate one's beliefs without hindrance. Whether with historical accuracy or not, American Protestantism proudly considers religious freedom the peculiar creation of Protestantism and cannot conceive of any society or any set of circumstances that would justify restrictions on freedom to worship and freedom to preach and teach in accordance with the dictates of conscience.

American Judaism is also fully committed to religious freedom. It, too, has completely and happily adjusted itself to the libertarianism of the alliance. With the exception of a small Orthodox fringe, it avows a commitment in principle as well as in practice, and does not approve such infringements on religious freedom as may be practiced in Israel. Judaism takes its own particular pride in religious freedom, asserting that the war of the Jews under the Maccabees against the Seleucids in the second century before Christ was the first recorded struggle for religious freedom.

In America only Catholicism is faced with the problem of reconciling with the libertarian ideal dogmatic pronouncements antipathetic to that ideal and to American concepts of religious freedom. This it seeks to do by drawing a distinction between a theoretical completely Catholic state and an actual pluralistic America. Many non-Catholics remain skeptical and consider Catholic avowals of acceptance of the American libertarian ideal as merely a compromise of expediency. Catholics recognize this skepticism, and realize the difficulty of their position. However, they see no alternative other than abandoning their belief that Catholicism is the one religion founded by Jesus Christ for all, and this they are not prepared to do.

Catholics urge that their differences with non-Catholics on the subject of religious freedom are purely differences of theory, having no practical relevance to the American scene. In one respect, however, the differences are not academic and have practical and tangible consequences. The statements of position of organized Protestantism and Judaism include within the mantle of protection of religious freedom the non-religious, and even the anti-religious. Catholic churchmen show no sympathy to this view. Throughout their writings one discerns a complete absence of tolerance for those who are "against God." Religious freedom belongs to those who are religious. The First Amendment secures freedom "of religion," not freedom "from religion"; the purpose of the guaranty is to protect the citizens in the exercise of their religion, not in the exercise of irreligion. The basic difference between America and Soviet Russia lies in the acceptance or rejection of God, and any American who rejects God is potentially if not actually an enemy of the nation and as such certainly has no right to teach and propagate his evil doctrines. American Catholicism sees no material difference between atheism and communism, and deems it the obligation of the government and the people to defend themselves equally against both evils.

SEPARATION OF CHURCH AND STATE

The principle of religious freedom and the separation of church and state—the latter phrase was coined by Jefferson—is as uniquely American a concept and experiment as anything can be said to be. A system of society wherein the secular state lacked jurisdiction over the relationship of man to God or the gods was certainly without precedent in human history. It had never occurred to any but a few visionaries that it might be wrong for a secular ruler to dictate to his subjects how they should worship God or for priests to dictate to the state how it should conduct its secular affairs. It was the United States alone that conceived and proved the workability of the idea that, as Lord Bryce put it, religious organizations should be "unrecognized by law except as voluntary associations of private citizens."

The principle of freedom and separation was based upon the dual concept of voluntariness in matters of belief and government without inherent powers but limited to those specifically conferred upon it. It was given a constitutional protection in the opening words of the Bill of Rights: "Congress shall make no law respecting an establishment of religion, or prohibiting the free exercise thereof." This came about because in 1791, when the Bill of Rights (the first ten amendments to the Constitution) was adopted, the two most potent cultural forces in America were Protestant dissent and secular humanism; both were committed to it, and they combined to establish it as a fundamental principle of the American political system.

The concept of voluntariness in matters of belief has been called the great tradition of the American churches. More properly, it is the great tradition of the American dissenting churches. It is also the tradition of the secular-humanist political leaders who shared in the establishment of our democratic system. Their writings contain innumerable references to the evil, tyranny, and inefficacy of coercion in the realm of conscience. Both also agreed that political government has only such powers as are delegated to it and that the power to intervene in religious affairs was not granted to political government. Hence, the new government then being established should have no power to make any law respecting an establishment of religion or prohibiting its free exercise.

The two groups arrived at the common ideological meeting place from different directions. To the leaders of Protestant dissent the source of all temporal power was God, and He had not seen fit to delegate power over religion to temporal governments. The Baptist Roger Williams pointed out that the Ten Commandments were written by God on two tablets. On one side were the commandments which concern man's relation to God, e.g., "Thou shalt have no other gods before me," "Thou shalt not make unto thee any graven image," etc. On the other side were those concerning man's relationship to man, e.g., "Thou shalt not kill," etc. By placing a line of demarcation between the two tablets, God expressed His wish that transgressions of obligations between man and man shall be subject to the jurisdiction of man's tribunals, but the relationship of man to God shall be exclusively within God's jurisdiction.

A later Baptist leader, Samuel Stayman, preached that the "jurisdiction of the magistrate neither can nor ought to be extended to the salvation of souls." John Leland, Baptist leader in Virginia, wrote a tract in the same year that the First Amendment was adopted, entitled "Rights of Conscience and therefore Religious Opinions not recognizable by law." In this tract Leland said that "government has no more to do with religious opinions of man than with the principles of mathematics." Isaac Backus, spokesman for the Massachusetts Baptist Churches at the time of the Revolutionary War and the Constitution, in arguing against the use of tax-raised funds for religious purposes, said: "The free exercise of private judgment and the inalienable rights of consciences are too high a rank and dignity to be submitted to the decrees of councils or the imperfect laws of fallible legislators. . . . Religion is a concern between God and the soul with which no human authority can intermeddle. . . ." And a few years before adoption of the First Amendment, another important segment of American Protestant dissent, the Presbyterian Church, argued against taxation for religious purposes on the ground that

The end of Civil government is security to the temporal liberty and property of Mankind; and to protect them in the free Exercise of Religion—Legislators are invested with powers from their constituents, for these purposes only; and their duty extends no further—Religion is altogether personal, and the right of exercising it unalienable; and it is not, cannot, and ought not to be, resigned to the will of society at large; and much less to the Legislature—which derives its authority wholly from the consent of the people; and is limited to the Original intention of Civil Associations.

The last quotation shows clearly the alliance between Protestant dissent and rationalist humanism, for it reflects the social contract theory of Locke and Rousseau. This theory was widely accepted in the latter half of the eighteenth century and upon it was based the Declaration of Independence and the American libertarian system of democratic government. According to the theory of the social contract, governments, in the words of the Declaration of Independence, "are instituted among men, deriving their just powers from the consent of the governed." A government, therefore, has only such powers as are granted to it by the governed, and if it seeks to exercise powers not granted to it, it is guilty of tyranny and usurpation.

The rationalists and deists who found their inspiration in the social contract believed that, as Madison put it, "in matters of religion no man's right is abridged by the institution of civil society, and that religion is wholly exempt from its cognizance." The reason for this, they argued, is that matters of conscience are by their very nature inalienable, and therefore jurisdiction over them was not and could not have been delegated to political government in the social contract. The views of this group were epitomized in Paine's statement in *Common Sense:* "As to religion, I hold it to be the indispensable duty of government to protect all conscientious professors thereof; and I know of no other business which government hath to do therewith."

In 1786, but one short year before the Federal Constitutional Convention met in Philadelphia, Protestant dissent and rationalist humanism joined forces to defeat a bill introduced in Virginia whose purpose was to provide tax funds for the teaching of religion. The major factor in the defeat of the bill was Madison's "Memorial and Remonstrance," which set forth fifteen arguments against the measure. These arguments fell principally into two classes: those predicated on the concept of voluntariness in matters of conscience, and those on the concept that religion is outside the jurisdiction of political government—the two aspects of what five years later was to become the religion clause of the First Amendment. Immediately on defeat of the bill, the alliance put through Jefferson's great Virginia Statute Establishing Religious Freedom which also reflected the dual concept of voluntariness and no-jurisdiction.

Flushed with success, the alliance had no real difficulty a year later in keeping out of the proposed Federal Constitution any invocation or even reference to God, and in making that instrument a purely secular document whose listed purposes carefully excluded anything pertaining to religion. In fact, the only reference to religion in the entire document was the negative one prohibiting religious tests for Federal office, a provision that the drafters fully realized could open the door for "Jews, Turks and infidels" to become President. Other than this no provision guaranteeing religious liberty was expressly stated, the reason being that such a provision was believed unnecessary since the Federal government would in any event have no jurisdiction in religious affairs. This explanation, however, proved unsatisfactory, and four years later the First Amendment was added to the Constitution expressly barring laws respecting an establishment of religion or prohibiting its free exercise, i.e., no-jurisdiction and voluntariness.

THE MEANING OF THE NO-ESTABLISHMENT CLAUSE

For more than a century and a half the United States Supreme Court had no occasion to spell out definitively the meaning of the no-establishment clause—itself a silent yet significant witness to the effectiveness of the Protestant dissent-secular humanist alliance in shaping American politico-cultural patterns. It was only when in the mid-twentieth century the dominance of the alliance was challenged by Roman Catholicism that the Court was called upon to determine whether the no-establishment clause had made the philosophy of the alliance the supreme law of the land. It was no coincidence that the issue should reach the Supreme Court in a case involving a Roman Catholic attack upon the principle established by the alliance that tax-raised funds must not be used in support of religion.

This occurred in 1947 in the famous parochial school bus case, *Everson* v. *Board of Education*. In that case, while upholding by a vote of five to four the validity of using tax-raised funds to transport children to parochial schools, the Court spelled out the meaning of the First Amendment in the following definitive language:

> *The "establishment of religion" clause of the First Amendment means at least this: Neither a state nor the Federal Government can set up a church. Neither can pass laws which aid one religion, aid all religions, or prefer one religion over another. Neither can force nor influence a person to go to or to remain away from church against his will or force him to profess a belief or disbelief in any religion. No person can be punished for entertaining or professing religious beliefs or disbeliefs, for church attendance or non-attendance. No tax in any amount, large or small, can be levied to support any religious activities or institutions, whatever they may be called, or whatever form they may adopt to teach or practice religion. Neither a state nor the Federal Government can, openly or secretly, participate in the affairs of any religious organizations or groups and vice versa. In the words of Jefferson, the clause against establishment of religion by law was intended to erect "a wall of separation between Church and State."*

This statement, which was reiterated by the Supreme Court the following year in the McCollum released-time case, shows clearly that the Court had interpreted the First Amendment as conferring the force of constitutional law on the principles of the Protestant dissent-secular humanist alliance. The statement imposes upon government an obligation to abstain from intervention in religious affairs and from granting governmental aid or support to religious institutions. As Lord Bryce had earlier noted, it expresses the view that in the United States religious associations are merely voluntary associations of private persons whose activities must be considered by the government as exclusively private and not subject to support out of tax-raised funds. It imposes an obligation of neutrality on government not merely as between different religions but also as between religion and non-religion, and indeed between religion and anti-religion.

That, said the Supreme Court, is what the fathers of the Constitution and of the First Amendment intended. And they intended it not because they were hostile to religion; the fact that the deeply pietistic dissenting sects strove for this is conclusive proof that its motivation was not unfriendliness to religion. The fathers of our republic, said the Court, were convinced that the cause of religion could best be served if the government maintained a strict hands-off policy and if it maintained a high and impregnable wall between church and state. They were convinced too that the best way to keep from these shores the religious bloodshed, persecution, and intolerance that had plagued the old world was to maintain such a wall between church and state in the new world.

This definitive interpretation of the no-establishment clause evoked considerable criticism from a number of sources. It was argued that the Supreme Court had misread the Constitution and had misinterpreted the intent of its framers. It was not the purpose of the First Amendment to divorce religion from government or to impose neutrality between believers and non-believers but only to meet in a practical manner the problems raised by a multiplicity of competing sects. This was done by requiring the government to be neutral as among these sects and forbidding it to favor one at the expense of the others. The amendment was not intended to bar the government from aiding and supporting religion and religious institutions so long as the aid and support is granted equally and without preference to some faiths and discrimination against others.

The proof of this, according to the critics of the Supreme Court's interpretation, is to be found in the history of our country and in the society about us. Throughout its history our governments, national and state, have co-operated with religion and shown friendliness to it. God is invoked in the Declaration of Independence and in practically every state constitution. Sunday, the Christian Sabbath, is universally observed as a day of rest. The sessions of Congress and of the state legislatures are invariably opened with prayer, in Congress by chaplains who are employed by the Federal government. We have chaplains in our armed forces and in our penal institutions. Oaths in courts of law are administered through use of the Bible. Public officials take an oath of office ending with "so help me God." Religious institutions are tax exempt throughout the nation.

Our Pledge of Allegiance declares that we are a nation "under God." Our national motto is "In God We Trust" and is inscribed on our currency and our postage stamps.

These and many other similar illustrations of governmental co-operation with religion, say the critics of the Everson-McCollum principle, show conclusively that the purpose of the First Amendment was not to erect an absolute, unpenetrable wall between religion and government nor to make our nation Godless. The amendment, they say, prohibits preferential treatment and imposes an obligation of neutrality on the part of government as among the different religious groups, but not as between religion and non-religion, nor as between God-fearers and atheists.

The intensive criticism the Everson-McCollum principle received during the four years between the McCollum case and the New York City released-time case, *Zorach* v. *Clauson*, quite likely influenced the Supreme Court. For the decision in the Zorach case shows some retreat from the broad scope of the Everson-McCollum principle. "We are," said the Court, "a religious people whose institutions presuppose a Supreme Being." The First Amendment "does not say that in every and all respects there shall be a separation of Church and State." It requires only that "there shall be no concert or union or dependency one on the other."

Despite this language, it is doubtful that the Zorach decision is to be interpreted as a repudiation of the Everson-McCollum principle. The Court expressly stated that it adhered to the McCollum decision, a decision which, as we shall see in the next chapter, is consistent only with the broad interpretation of the First Amendment expressed in the Everson and McCollum cases. The Court in the Zorach case also went out of its way to say that under the First Amendment "Government may not finance religious groups nor undertake religious instruction"—a disability required only if the broad interpretation of the Everson and McCollum cases is accepted.

It is clear from this that the difference as to the intention of the fathers of the First Amendment and of the meaning of the amendment is not a mere academic exercise in American history. The difference in interpretation has practical consequences of tremendous importance. If the amendment is interpreted narrowly to prohibit only preferential aid, then it is permissible for Congress and the states to appropriate public funds for the support of religious education so long as all church schools are included in the program without favoritism or discrimination. Also it is permissible for the public schools to teach religion so long as each child is taught his own religion or the common elements of the major religions are taught to all children. If the broad Everson-McCollum interpretation is followed, neither government financing of religious education nor religious instruction in the public schools is permissible.

These practical consequences explain the differences among the religious faiths on the correctness or incorrectness of the Supreme Court's interpretation of the First Amendment. That religious groups should divide on this might seem strange at first sight. One would suppose that while historians could well differ as to a particular historical fact such as the intent of the fathers of our Constitution, the difference would not be reflected in, much less determined by, the difference in their religious affiliations. So too, while lawyers and law professors might differ as to the correct interpretation of a constitutional provision, that difference would seem to bear no logical relationship to whether they are Protestant, Catholic, or Jewish. Yet it is not as surprising as it would seem at first. It is human to read history and the Constitution as one would want history and the Constitution to be, and the deeper the want the more convinced one is that the interpretation is correct. In any event, the differences among (and, in the case of Protestantism, within) the religious groups as to the meaning of the First Amendment and separation of church and state reflect completely their diverse positions on specific practical issues of public importance, as well as their differences in accepting or challenging the political and cultural patterns shaped by the alliance of Protestant dissent and secular humanism.

CHURCH AND STATE IN CATHOLICISM

Even more than religious liberty, the notion that church and state should be separated and political government be secular is alien to Catholic dogma. For Catholicism a secular state is by its very nature a denial of God, since the supremacy of God requires that He be acknowledged and worshiped by all that He created, including the rulers of states. In speaking of the duty of government officials to profess and practice God's revealed religion, Pope Pius XI stated that there is no "difference in this matter between individuals and societies, both domestic and civil; for men joined in society are no

less under the power of Christ than individuals." Catholic dogma on
the relation of church and state was thus expressed by Leo XIII:

Justice therefore forbids, and reason itself forbids, the State to be god-
less; or to adopt a line of action which would end in godlessness—namely,
to treat the various religions (as they call them) alike, and to bestow upon
them promiscuously equal rights and privileges. Since, then, the profession
of one religion is necessary in the State, that religion must be professed
which alone is true, and which can be recognized without difficulty, espe-
cially in Catholic States, because the marks of truth are, as it were, en-
graven upon it. This religion, therefore, the rulers of the State must
preserve and protect, if they would provide—as they should do—with
prudence and usefulness for the good of the community.

As in the case of religious freedom, Catholic churchmen in the
United States explain that these principles, though valid in theory,
are inapplicable to a multi-religious society such as exists in America.
Here the state cannot be expected, nor is it required, to acknowledge
the exclusive truthfulness of the Catholic faith or to accord that
faith sole or even preferential recognition. It is permissible for the
state to conduct its affairs as if all religions were equally true, or,
perhaps more accurately, it is permissible for the state not to pass
judgment on which religion is the only true one. Hence, it is permissible for the state to bestow its favors and privileges equally upon
all accepted religions.

This does not mean that the state even in America may be secular
or Godless. On the contrary, American governments are as obligated
to recognize the existence and supremacy of God through public
and official acts of acknowledgment and worship as are governments
in Catholic states. Catholicism holds that all governments, including those representative of populations of many sects, are morally
obliged to engage in official acts of state worship and state acknowledgment of God. To this aspect of Catholic belief and to the growing influence of such belief on American culture can largely be
attributed the recent manifestation of religion on the part of our
government and our government officials, from the public religiosity
of President Eisenhower and his aides to the inclusion of "under
God" in the Pledge of Allegiance.

It is immediately obvious that the broad interpretation of the First
Amendment expounded in the Everson and McCollum cases is com-

pletely incompatible with Catholic dogma, even as adjusted for application in non-Catholic states. It is also obvious that the narrow interpretation which would limit the meaning of the amendment to a ban on preferential treatment of any one faith is admirably in harmony with Catholic doctrine on the relationship of religion and government in non-Catholic states. It is therefore less than surprising that American Catholicism should vigorously oppose the Everson-McCollum principle and with equal vigor urge that the narrow interpretation of the First Amendment is the only valid one. Nor is it surprising that Catholic churchmen and spokesmen should indicate a strong dislike for the phrase "separation of church and state," calling it at various times a "shibboleth," "fraudulent," "un-American," etc., preferring to frame their arguments in terms of the no-establishment clause of the First Amendment.

The most authoritative expression of the Catholic position is to be found in a statement issued by the Catholic bishops through the National Catholic Welfare Conference several months after the McCollum decision was handed down in 1948. The statement, which is too long to be set forth here in full, declared:

To one who knows something of history and law, the meaning of the First Amendment is clear enough from its own words: "Congress shall make no laws (sic) respecting an establishment of religion or forbidding (sic) the free exercise thereof." The meaning is even clearer in the records of the Congress that enacted it. Then and throughout English and Colonial history "an establishment of religion" meant the setting up by law of an official Church which would receive from the government favors not equally accorded to others in the cooperation between government and religion—which was simply taken for granted in our country at that time and has, in many ways, continued to this day. Under the First Amendment, the Federal Government could not extend this type of preferential treatment to one religion as against another, nor could it compel or forbid any state to do so.

If this practical policy be described by the loose metaphor "a wall of separation between Church and State," that term must be understood in a definite and typically American sense. It would be an utter distortion of American history and law to make that practical policy involve the indifference to religion and the exclusion of cooperation between religion and government implied in the term "separation of Church and State" as it has become the shibboleth of doctrinaire secularism. . . .

We, therefore, hope and pray that the novel interpretation of the First Amendment recently adopted by the Supreme Court will in due process be revised. To that end we shall peacefully, patiently and perseveringly work. . . .

We call upon all Catholic people to seek in their faith an inspiration and a guide in making an informed contribution to good citizenship. We urge members of the legal profession in particular to develop and apply their special competence in this field. We stand ready to cooperate in fairness and charity with all who believe in God and are devoted to freedom under God to avert the impending danger of a judicial "establishment of secularism" that would ban God from public life.

The substance of this statement of the Catholic position has been repeated countless times by Catholic churchmen and spokesmen. I have not found a single Catholic cleric or Catholic publication that dissents from it. The unanimity with which these views are held among American Catholics and the vigor with which they are defended make it fatuous to argue that there is no "Catholic" position on separation of church and state and the meaning of the First Amendment.

SEPARATION AND AMERICAN JEWRY

As it is not surprising that American Catholicism found the narrow interpretation of the First Amendment to be the only true and valid one, so it is no more astonishing that American Judaism found the broad interpretation expressed in the Everson and McCollum decisions to be the only true and valid one. For, as we have seen, Judaism happily adjusted itself to the American libertarianism which was articulated in the Everson-McCollum principle.

Because of the structural differences between Catholicism and Judaism, it is not to be expected that the same unanimity will be found in Judaism as in Catholicism. There are, undoubtedly, some rabbis who agree with Will Herberg, Jewish professor of theology at Drew University, and with the Catholic Church that the Everson-McCollum principles do not correctly reflect American traditions, nor the true American spirit, which is religious rather than secular. At least, one finds dissent among the rabbinate where no dissent is to be found among the Catholic priesthood.

It remains true, however, that there is substantial unanimity in American Judaism in support of the broad interpretation of the First Amendment announced by the Supreme Court in the Everson and McCollum cases. In 1955, a subcommittee of the United States Senate Committee on the Judiciary, under the chairmanship of Senator Thomas C. Hennings, Jr., of Missouri, instituted a study of the status of constitutional rights in the nation. Among the questions investigated was the extent of public agreement or disagreement with the Supreme Court's interpretation of the First Amendment in the Everson and McCollum cases. A statement of views was submitted to the committee by the Synagogue Council of America, consisting of and representing the six national organizations that comprise organized American Judaism—Reform, Conservative, and Orthodox, both at the rabbinic and congregational levels. In its statement, the Synagogue Council expressed its conviction "that the provision against establishment of religion in the First Amendment bars non-preferential as well as preferential aid to religion," and that "the First and Fourteenth Amendments impose upon government in American democracy an obligation of strict separation, an obligation that precludes all material aid to religion by Congress and the states whether accorded on a preferential or non-preferential basis."

The statement pointed out that when the McCollum case was before the Supreme Court and the broad interpretation announced in the Everson case was under attack, the Synagogue Council, representing American Judaism, had submitted a brief as "friend of the court" urging the Supreme Court not to retreat from the broad interpretation. Since then, whenever the Synagogue Council expressed a statement of policy in areas where religion and government meet and interact, the Council has consistently reiterated its adherence to the Everson-McCollum principles and to the broad interpretation of the First Amendment.

Organized Jewry has not expressed itself publicly on the numerous governmental manifestations of religiosity such as including "under God" in the Pledge of Allegiance or putting "Pray for Peace" on postage stamp cancelations. That not a single member of either House of Congress voted against any of these measures is good evidence that it is not politic to be "against God," a reality which even the rationalist Jefferson recognized and took into account. The silence of American Jewry, a minority that is just beginning to enjoy equality of status, is therefore understandable. Yet it is safe to say that most Jewish organizations, religious as well as secular, are not happy about the increasing religious coloration of governmental action.

THE PROTESTANT DILEMMA

The position of American Protestantism in respect to the meaning and scope of the First Amendment is neither as definite nor as uniform as that of Catholicism and Judaism. Protestantism is faced with a dilemma. On the one hand most Protestant groups, even such denominations as Congregationalism and Episcopalianism which vigorously but vainly fought disestablishment, today claim the principle of separation of church and state as a purely Protestant creation. They deem it a great contribution to America and to Western civilization generally, and are extremely proud of it. Also they assert the principle as the basis for, and justification of, their almost unanimous opposition to such measures as the grant of tax-raised funds to parochial schools or to an exchange of ambassadors with the Vatican. At the same time most Protestant organizations are committed to compulsory Sunday observance laws, to certain aspects of religious education in connection with the public school system (such as released-time programs and Bible readings), and to other instances of governmental aid to religion which cannot easily be reconciled with the broad interpretation of the First Amendment announced in the Everson and McCollum decisions.

The offspring of the Protestant dilemma is ambivalence and the offspring of ambivalence are ambiguity and confusion and not a little self-deception. Compulsory Sunday observance laws are defended as health rather than religious measures, even though their chief defenders are such unsecular organizations as the Lord's Day Alliance and the Catholic Church. There is some flirting with the narrow interpretation of the amendment when Protestants argue that an exchange of ambassadors with the Vatican would be a preferential treatment of the Catholic Church, although, as they quickly point out, Protestant opposition would not be disposed of by adding an exchange of representatives with the World Council of Churches. The same sort of flirtation appears in the argument that public aid to parochial schools would constitute preferential treatment of the Catholic Church, although it is not explained why Protestants and

Jews cannot establish their own parochial schools (as indeed they have to a small extent) and share equally in the state's favor.

Most Protestants recognize, even if they do not admit, the unavoidable dilemma and the basic self-contradiction of their specific positions. A few on the left will express outright approval of the broad interpretation with full understanding and acceptance of its implications and consequences on such specifics as Sunday laws and religion in the public schools. A few on the right, on the other hand, will approve the narrow interpretation with full understanding and acceptance of its implications and consequences on such specifics as representation at the Vatican and grant of tax-raised funds to parochial schools.

The majority solve the dilemma by pretending it does not exist. They simply avoid expressing a definite position on the scope of the First Amendment and the meaning of separation of church and state. The Senate Judiciary subcommittee had no doubts about the Catholic position on the question, nor about the Jewish position. But it must have been quite perplexed as to what the Protestant position is. The National Council of Churches, in its statement submitted to the subcommittee, simply disregarded the pointedly worded question put by the subcommittee and stated its position in the following characteristically ambiguous language:

The National Council of Churches holds the first clause of the First Amendment to the Constitution of the United States to mean that church and state shall be separate and independent as institutions, but to imply neither that the state is indifferent to religion nor that the church is indifferent to civil and political issues.

It is at least probable that most Protestant clergymen and organizations approve the recent overt manifestations of religiosity on the part of government in the United States. Moreover, even among the minority that disapproves, disapproval is predicated not so much on considerations of church-state relations as on the questionable value and sincerity of such superficial verbalizations. A few Protestant voices, however, have indicated uneasiness on constitutional grounds. The extent of Protestant disapproval cannot be gauged by the volume of articulated objection, for it is almost as difficult for Protestants to be publicly "against God" as it is for Jews.

4. GOD AND THE SCHOOLS

PROTESTANTISM AND PUBLIC EDUCATION

No contemporary issue on the American scene divides the major faiths more seriously than does the role of the public school system in religious education. This is quite understandable, for the public schools are the chief instrument for forming our cultural patterns and for transmitting them from generation to generation, so that the power that controls our public schools in large measure controls our culture. Hence, in the competition among religious cultures the public school system must necessarily be the most sought after prize.

The American public school system is the great offspring of the alliance between Protestantism and secular humanism. The Protestantism in this case is not Protestant dissent alone but Protestant dissent along with New England Congregationalism; indeed, the role of the latter was probably more significant and, in any event, prior in time. The aristocracy of Virginian Anglicanism had little use for universal education and made no significant contribution to the evolution and development of America's public educational system. Anglicanism, closest to Roman Catholicism in dogma, ritual, and general spirit, found no need for universal literacy; of all Protestant denominations it was most episcopal, most ritualistic, and least Bible-centered.

The situation in New England was radically different. Government there was based on Congregational Church policy; it was a theocratic commonwealth founded on the Bible. Familiarity with the Bible was a requirement of citizenship, and familiarity presupposed the ability to read it. Literacy, therefore, was a religious obligation as much as

57.

a secular one, if not more so. It was natural, therefore, that the first compulsory education law in America should have been enacted in Puritan Massachusetts as early as 1642 and that one of its purposes should be that children should acquire the "ability to read and understand the principles of religion." It was natural too that the Massachusetts law of 1647, which established the base for the American system of compulsory elementary education by imposing upon all municipalities the obligation to conduct schools, should state as its preamble and purpose:

> *It being the chief project of that old deluder, Satan, to keep men from the knowledge of the Scriptures, as in former times by keeping them in an unknown tongue, so in these later times by persuading from the use of tongues, that so at least the true sense and meaning of the original might be clouded by false glosses of saint-seeming deceivers, that learning may not be buried in the graves of our fathers in the church and commonwealth. . . .*

Protestant dissent, an even more Bible-centered religion than New England Calvinism, found it equally necessary to foil "that old deluder, Satan," by insuring that every believer should be able to read the Bible for himself without the "false glosses of saint-seeming deceivers." It therefore likewise felt the urgency of securing universal literacy. Frontier conditions naturally made communal schooling difficult at first and imposed upon parents the responsibility for educating their children, but as soon as conditions permitted, village and town schools were established and maintained by the community for the children of all.

Of course, secular humanism, with its egalitarian spirit and its faith in reason, was quick to espouse the cause of universal education, although, to be sure, for far different motives. Jefferson, the intellectual leader of rationalist humanism, devoted much of his writings to the cause of universal education controlled by civic authorities. "If," said Jefferson, "the condition of man is to be progressively ameliorated, as we fondly hope and believe, education is to be the chief instrument in effecting it." The optimism of secular humanism and its faith in the potency of reason and education is indicated by his dictum: "Enlighten the people generally, and tyranny and oppression of body and mind will vanish like evil spirits at the dawn of day."

Jefferson's influence in the South made up only in part for the apathy of the Anglican Church toward education for any but the children of the aristocracy. The pattern of American common school education was fixed in Puritan New England, and Protestantism may with some justice claim as indeed it does, to be the father of the American public school system. Not that it has been entirely happy with the secularization of the public educational system, which developed as we shall shortly see, out of a strange alliance among dissent, secular humanism, and Roman Catholicism. But so committed has Protestantism been to the public school system that, until very recently at least, it was willing to pay the price of secularity for its preservation. It is probably also true that given the choice today between a secular public school system and none at all, most Protestants would choose the secular school. Whether they will long continue so to choose is, however, by no means certain.

AMERICAN JEWRY AND THE PUBLIC SCHOOLS

American Jewry has happily enjoyed the fruits of the alliance between Protestantism and secular humanism, and of all the fruits it has been most happy with the public school system. Like Protestantism, Judaism is a Bible-centered religion which views the obligation to read and understand the Bible (Torah) as resting upon all Jews. Jewry therefore has always placed a high premium on universal literacy, and the communal obligation to provide schools for all children has been a characteristic of Judaism for well over two thousand years. These schools, to be sure, were religious and not secular institutions. Indeed, Talmudic Judaism discouraged study of secular, and particularly Gentile, learning. But with the emancipation of Jewry from the Ghetto, which began with the twin triumphs of secular humanism—the French Revolution in Europe and the establishment of constitutional libertarianism in America—the long pent-up longing for the wisdom and learning of all peoples broke out to embrace the American public educational system with a devotion unmatched even by Protestantism.

There is another reason for this intense commitment to the public school system on the part of American Jewry. By the time Jews began coming to this country in substantial numbers at the turn of the twentieth century, the secularization of the public educational system had been completed. The overwhelming majority of Jews came from Czarist Russia and Poland. Jewish children fortunate enough to gain admittance to the government schools in those countries experienced daily the whiplash of official anti-Semitism and were never allowed to forget their inferior status. Moreover, the schools were pervaded with Christian teachings, ritual, and prayer, all of which the Jewish child had to endure in uncomplaining but unhappy silence.

When the Jewish immigrant came to America he found that the government school not only tolerated his child but actually welcomed him. He found too that his child was treated as the complete equal of all other children and that this equality of treatment was the proud boast of the school authorities. He found, finally, that except for some sporadic and often purely perfunctory reading of a few verses from the Bible, the schools were generally devoid of the Christological religiosity that so discomfited him in eastern Europe.

The Jewish immigrant, and his children on attaining adulthood and parenthood, would have been other than human if they had not seen in the American public school system a precious gift to be passionately protected and preserved. It is chiefly for these reasons that the American public school system finds its stanchest defenders within the Jewish community.

CATHOLICISM AND COMMON EDUCATION

The Bible does not enjoy the centrality of importance in Catholicism that it does in Protestantism and Judaism. According to Catholic dogma, the Church is not the child of the Bible but its mother. It was the Church that created the Bible, and the Church was created by Jesus, who neither wrote the Bible or anything else, nor commanded his disciples to write anything. Catholicism, moreover, denies the capacity of its laity to interpret the Bible, and for centuries discouraged reading of the Bible by any but the priesthood. Although today the Catholic laity are encouraged to read the Bible, it remains true that obedience to the Church, attendance at rites, and the recitation of easily memorized prayers are still considered more important obligations than Bible reading.

The subordinate role of the Bible in Catholicism explains the secondary importance of universal literacy and hence universal education in the Catholic scheme of the ideal society. It is significant that revolts from Catholicism—by Protestantism in northern Europe, rationalism in France, or radical agrarianism in Mexico—have almost invariably been accompanied by a surge toward common education and the eradication of illiteracy.

Besides the general apathy if not antipathy of the Catholic Church toward universal education, it has for a long time shown special unfriendliness to the American public school system. For many years the attitude of the Catholic Church to the public school alternated between indifference and open hostility. The adversaries of the Catholic Church in America—Paul Blanshard, Protestants and Other Americans United for Separation of Church and State, *The Converted Catholic Magazine* [1] among others—delight in quoting from the writings of Catholic churchmen expressing antagonism to the public school system.

Catholic hostility to the public schools arose out of the bitter experiences that Catholic children suffered in them. When Jews began to come to this country in large numbers, the secularization of the schools had already been completed; when the Catholics first came in numbers it was just beginning. The transition from a Protestant to a secular school system was a difficult one in the course of which there arose considerable tension and friction. Catholic children were the principal victims. For refusing to participate in Protestant religious exercises or the reading of the Protestant Bible, Catholic public school children frequently suffered cruel persecution. They were often subjected to physical punishment, expulsion, and other indignities merely because they took seriously the guaranty of religious freedom of which the Protestants so proudly boasted. The transition from Protestant to secular public education, moreover, took place during a period when anti-Catholic bigotry was strong and extensive, when Nativism and Know-Nothingism flourished over a large part of the country. The child of the Jewish immigrant from Russia and Poland came from a background of persecution, discrimination, and bigotry to a public school of acceptance and equality. The child of the Catholic immigrant from Ireland came from a climate of equality to a public school of persecution, discrimination, and bigotry. The difference in attitudes toward the public school on the part of the Catholic and Jewish communities hardly needs any other explanation.

---

[1] Now called *Christian Heritage.*

Catholic dogma on interreligious schools is another factor in shaping the Catholic attitude to American public education. Catholic Canon Law and numerous papal statements emphasize, as stated in the encyclical of Pius XI "On the Christian Education of Youth," that "the frequenting of non-Catholic schools, whether neutral or mixed, those namely which are open to Catholics and non-Catholics alike, is forbidden for Catholic children, and can at most be tolerated, on the approval of the Ordinary [bishop] alone, under determined circumstances of place and time, and with special precautions."

These, then, are the factors responsible for the attitude of the Catholic Church to the nation's public educational system, an attitude that progressed from deep antagonism to indifference. Recently, however, the Church has begun to show a growing interest in the public schools. Not that the Church has altered its dogmatic position against non-Catholic education for Catholic children, nor that it has abandoned its goal of placing every Catholic child in a Catholic school. On the contrary, it has embarked on an ambitious school-building campaign to bring that goal nearer to realization. Nevertheless, the Church has lately shown an increasing interest in what happens within the public school classrooms. No longer is its interest in the curriculum and internal operations of the public school limited to the protection of Catholic children from Protestant teachings and proselytization. The era of Church indifference is rapidly changing to one of great concern.

A concrete indication is the increasing number of instances when the Catholic Church has involved itself in the choice, through appointment or election, of members of boards of education. In New York City the nine members of the Board of Education are apportioned equally among the three faiths, and it is certain that the Catholic Church exercises a veto power, if it does not directly designate, the three Catholic members. Today in many communities, priests and nuns vote in the elections for members of the boards of education; church newspapers and magazines take active parts in the campaigns and priests sermonize from the pulpit on the issues, leaving the congregation with little doubt as to whom to vote for. In fact, priests are themselves beginning to seek and accept membership on public school boards of education. These are events which were almost inconceivable as recently as two or three decades ago. Yet today they are rapidly becoming commonplace.

What is the explanation for this startling turn of events? Is it the realization that notwithstanding the strenuous efforts of the Church to expand its parochial school system, some 50 per cent of Catholic children still attend elementary public schools, with an even larger percentage in secondary public schools, so that the achievement of the goal of having every Catholic child in a Catholic school lies beyond the foreseeable future? The large number of Catholic children in the public schools is the explanation frequently urged by Catholic spokesmen to support their denial of charges of Catholic hostility to the public school system. Undoubtedly there is some validity to the explanation; but I do not think it tells the whole story. Certainly it is strange that the realization that many Catholic children will continue indefinitely to attend public schools should come so suddenly at a time when the percentage of Catholic children attending Catholic schools is greater than ever and is steadily increasing.

The answer, I think, must be found in terms of cultural competition. The change of attitude coincided with the progress of Catholicism from its defensive role to becoming a vigorous and ambitious protagonist in the field of cultural competition. Catholicism, in its challenge to the Protestant-humanist alliance that has dominated American culture for a century and a half, recognizes that the country's school system has had a decided responsibility for the shaping of that culture. It recognizes that even if every Catholic child were in a Catholic school, the public educational system would still play a major role in determining the direction of American culture. It has seen its own cultural patterns affected by the Protestant-humanist culture, and the curricula, methods of pedagogy and philosophy of its own school system strongly influenced by the competition of the public school system. Catholicism is now ready not merely to halt this process but in some measure to reverse it. And Catholicism recognizes that one of the most effective areas for achieving this is in the public educational institutions.

It must be emphasized that there is nothing wrong or invidious about this. Except for purposes of Fourth of July oratory, our culture and our institutions are not to be considered God-given or God-fixed. Certainly American Catholicism does not and should not be compelled to believe that our Protestant-humanist society is exactly what God wants or is necessarily the best of all possible societies. The challenge by Catholicism is a healthful one, if for no other reason than that it calls upon those committed to our present social system to defend and justify it. Those pledged to the democratic proposition that the best test of truth is its ability to win acceptance in free and fair competition should welcome the competitive challenge of Catholicism. That is the American experiment.

THE SECULARIZATION OF THE SCHOOLS

The public schools established in colonial New England were religious schools. They were state institutions, but the state was identical with or, more accurately, subservient to the church. As Elwood P. Cubberly pointed out in his standard work, *Public Education in the United States*, it was the state acting as servant of the church that enacted the laws of 1642 and 1647 requiring the towns to maintain schools for religious purposes. The persons who controlled the schools and fixed their curriculum were the same persons who, as elders and deacons, controlled the church. Out of the church schools established by Congregational Protestantism in the seventeenth century New England evolved the American public school system of the nineteenth and twentieth centuries.

The first public schools were therefore religious schools and their secularization did not come about, at least initially, out of the efforts of the secular humanists. True enough, as early as 1779 Jefferson submitted to the Virginia legislature a plan for universal elementary education devoid of "religious reading, instruction or exercise." But Virginia's plantation aristocracy was not inclined toward universal education, and Jefferson's ideas were more important in the long-term shaping of American educational philosophy than in immediate practical results.

It was not out of secular humanism but out of Protestant dissent that came the first concrete steps toward the secularization of public education. The great contribution of Horace Mann in this development during the second quarter of the nineteenth century is well recognized. What is not equally well recognized is that Mann's efforts and successes represented the growing influence not of secular humanism but of Protestant dissent. Mann vigorously denied that he opposed religious instruction in the public schools. What he opposed and successfully fought against, he said, was sectarianism, and it was quite clear that by sectarianism he meant Calvinist theology. Bible religion, the common denominator of all Protestantism, was perfectly acceptable to Mann.

harmonious with the absolutist banner of separation of church and
state under which Protestant dissent had allied itself with secular
humanism in the framing and adoption of the First Amendment.
Hence some elements of Protestantism—liberal Unitarianism in the
North and some Baptists in the South—remained faithful to the tradition of dissent and joined secular humanism in its reluctance to
accept Mann's pan-Protestant solution as the final word. Most of
what had previously been Protestant dissent, however, was quite
willing to forget the alliance with secularism and enjoy the fruits of
a new, and in any event more comfortable, alliance with the formerly
established Congregationalism of New England and the formerly
established Anglicanism of Virginia.

Whether secular humanism and ultra-libertarian Protestant dissent
could alone have overcome the new pan-Protestant alliance and re-
sumed the march toward secularization of public education beyond
the point left by Mann can only be guessed. What we do know is
that success was achieved by reason of the entry into the fray of a
new and ever-more powerful combatant—the Roman Catholic community and the Roman Catholic Church. During the same period
that Mann was achieving his pan-Protestant *modus vivendi* there began a large-scale Catholic immigration from Ireland, to be followed
a little later by a large-scale Catholic immigration from south and
east Europe.

To the newcomers, the pan-Protestant compromise was not acceptable. To them the differences and nuances among Congregationalism, Episcopalianism, Methodism, Presbyterianism, etc. were of no
concern. Religious teaching based on and even limited to the Bible
violated their conscience where the Bible was the Protestant version
and the teaching Protestant teaching. Moreover, the newcomers sup-
plied what the secular humanists and the libertarian Protestant dissenters were apparently not ready to supply—a willingness to fight
and suffer for their convictions.

The struggle of the newly arrived Catholics for their right of conscience was indeed heroic and one without which the ultimate secularization of the American public educational system might never have been achieved. In community after community Catholic parents, on the urging of their priests, forbade their children to participate in Protestant religious instruction or exercise in the public schools. This they did notwithstanding the harassment and even persecution often visited upon their children by Protestant public school authorities. They went further. At the urging of their priests, they frequently went to court to challenge the legality of Protestant Bible instruction in the public schools.

Naturally, their goal was not the secularization of education; that concept was as unacceptable to Catholicism then as it is today. Their goal was to obtain for their parochial schools the same financial support out of tax-raised funds received by what they called the "Protestant public schools." The validity of their grievance could hardly be disputed by any but the most rabid anti-Catholic nativists and Know-Nothingers. The result was that American Protestantism was faced with the alternative of agreeing to state financing of Catholic teaching in Catholic schools or accepting the elimination of pan-Protestant teaching from state-financed schools. The choice was difficult, but one which could not be evaded.

For a time the issue was in doubt. In New York, for example, Governor William H. Seward, supported by a substantial segment of Protestantism, urged that public funds be appropriated for the support of schools in which Catholic children could be taught by teachers professing the same faith as they did. This solution, however, most of Protestantism would not accept. Faced with the unescapable dilemma, it chose what it considered the lesser evil: it accepted the elimination of pan-Protestantism from the schools. The secularization of American public education thus came about through a peculiar triple alliance of secular humanism, Roman Catholicism, and dissent within Protestant dissent. It is not only politics that makes strange bedfellows.

THE LAW, THE CONSTITUTION, AND THE
MCCOLLUM CASE

By the time the nineteenth century entered its fourth quarter the secularization of the American public educational system had been completed. Some vestiges of pan-Protestantism undoubtedly remained here and there. In the South, particularly in the rural areas, there were (and perhaps still are) quite a few public schools having many of the features of Bible schools. Even in the North many public schools retained an almost sentimental symbol of earlier times in the form of the daily reading of a few verses from the Bible. But by the beginning of the twentieth century, even these sporadic vestiges appeared on their way out. American public education had become secular education.

An attempt had been made during President Grant's administration to inscribe into the Federal Constitution the outcome of the strange alliance among secular humanism, libertarian Protestantism, and Roman Catholicism. An effort was made to amend the Constitution specifically to prohibit the use of public funds for religious education and the teaching of religion in the public schools. The proposal, though it obtained a majority, failed to win the necessary two-thirds vote in both houses of Congress and thus came to nought. But the defeat was no evidence that the objective of the measure was unacceptable to the American people. The evidence to the contrary was overwhelming and irrefutable. There was hardly a single state in the Union that did not by its laws or constitution forbid the use of tax-raised funds for religious schools or the involvement of the public schools in religious education.

The proposed amendment may have failed of passage because some of the senators who voted against it or obtained from voting for it felt that it was unnecessary. (It is more likely that it failed because it had become a matter of partisan politics. All senators who voted for it were Republicans; all who voted against it were Democrats.) In any event, what Congress in 1875 failed to achieve the Supreme Court effected three-quarters of a century later when in a period of a year it ruled in the Everson case that a state could not constitutionally use tax-raised funds to support parochial schools, and in the McCollum case that public schools could not undertake religious education. The Everson case will be discussed in the next chapter; here a brief consideration of the McCollum case is appropriate.

The McCollum case involved a suit by the mother of a child in the public schools of Champaign, Illinois, attacking a system in effect in the schools under which teachers of the various faiths came into the classrooms to instruct the children in their respective religions.

Because attendance at religious instruction was asserted to be completely voluntary, there was no infringement on freedom of religion. Since the doors of the school were open to teachers of all faiths on equal terms, there was no preferential treatment of some or discrimination against others. If, then, the narrow interpretation of the First Amendment discussed in the previous chapter were adopted, the Champaign system could not be ruled unconstitutional. The Supreme Court, however, refused to accept the narrow interpretation, and ruled that the program violated the First Amendment, since it involved the public schools in religious education.

The McCollum case and its aftermath mark the dissolution of the alliance that gave rise to the compromise by which public schools and public funds were secularized. The compromise, it will be remembered, was between pan-Protestantism and Roman Catholicism, the former yielding its claim to religious teaching in the public schools, and the latter its claim to public funds for its parochial schools. It was no compromise but a victory for secular humanism, for liberatarian Protestant dissent, and for Judaism; they gave up nothing, but on the contrary achieved a solution that they ardently desired. It was quite natural, therefore, that when the McCollum suit was brought (significantly, by a secular humanist) these forces should seek to defend their victory. Thus, briefs as "friend of the court" were filed in the McCollum case in support of Mrs. McCollum by the American Civil Liberties Union and the American Ethical Union (representatives of secular humanism), the Joint Baptist Committee on Public Affairs, the American Unitarian Association and the General Conference of Seventh Day Adventists (representatives of libertarian Protestant dissent), and the Synagogue Council of America (representative of all three branches of American Judaism).

Roman Catholicism, on the other hand, had become thoroughly discontented with the compromise which it had accepted a century earlier. It no longer feared religious teachings and exercises in the public schools; indeed, as we shall shortly see, it was rapidly becoming their chief advocate. Hence, it was bitterly disappointed with the McCollum decision, which not only put up a constitutional barrier against Catholic demands for public funds for its schools, but in addition read into the Constitution of the United States the way of life agreed upon by secular humanism and Protestant dissent. One who reads Catholic writings since 1948 cannot help noting that to the spokesmen for Catholicism the McCollum case is what the Dred Scott decision was to the Abolitionists in the years before the Civil War.

Pan-Protestantism (whose chief organ is the National Council of Churches) views the McCollum decision with uneasy ambivalence. In the latter part of the eighteenth century, when it was in the position of dissent, it joined forces with secular humanism to wage war against established Protestantism. After defeating and swallowing the established churches, it was ready to break off the alliance and enjoy the fruits of its victory, only to find itself faced by a new alliance of secular humanism, Roman Catholicism, and its own dissent. The Catholic declaration of war against the McCollum decision not only announced the breakup of this alliance, but was accompanied by an invitation to Protestantism to form a new alliance against secularism, and above all secularism in public education.

AFTERMATH OF MCCOLLUM—A NEW ALLIANCE?

Indications of the emergence of a new alliance began to appear shortly after the McCollum decision was announced, but perhaps the clearest evidence was revealed in the Zorach case. By its decision in the McCollum case the Supreme Court had rendered illegal programs involving religious instruction within public school classrooms under public school control and supervision. This decision sent the proponents of religious instruction in co-operation with public education on a search for permissible alternatives. The most promising of these appeared to be the released-time plan, under which children desiring to participate in religious instruction were excused from their secular studies for an hour or so each week to attend religious classes. The McCollum decision had held that these religious classes could not be conducted within the public school; it left unanswered the question whether they could be held outside the public school building but on public school time.

This question was answered in the Zorach decision, in which the Supreme Court upheld the constitutionality of a released-time program that did not involve public school participation beyond releasing the participating children from their secular studies for the period of religious instruction. What is particularly significant in the Zorach case is the composition of the antagonists. The suit to outlaw the released-time plan was sponsored and supported by the American Civil Liberties Union (secular humanism) and a number of Jewish organizations. It was opposed by the National Council of Churches (pan-Protestantism) and the Catholic Church. (The two chief defense counsels were a leading Protestant layman and the attorney for the Roman Catholic Archdiocese of New York.)

The released-time program had been a Protestant experiment originating before World War I. For some thirty years American Catholicism was indifferent to it. Few bishops bothered with it, preferring to concentrate the educational efforts of their dioceses on the parochial schools. With the McCollum decision the situation changed radically. The Catholic Church became the most ardent advocate of the released-time plan. More and more Catholic school systems began to participate in it. What was originally a pan-Protestant device quickly became a predominantly Catholic instrument, particularly in large urban areas. Today in New York City, for example, of every one hundred children released for religious instruction under the plan, about eighty are Catholic. In Chicago the percentage is approximately the same, as it probably is in other large cities where the plan is in operation. It is not too much to say that the released-time plan depends for its existence on Catholic support and that if the Catholic Church returned to its previous position of indifference and non-co-operation, the program would soon collapse.

Catholic change of position in respect to the released-time experiment is not difficult to understand. Catholicism allied itself with humanism and the remnants of Protestant dissent to secularize the public schools, not because it believed in the secularity of education —a concept totally unacceptable to Catholicism—but out of necessity, for the defense of its children in the public schools against Protestant instruction and proselytization. Released-time instruction off public school premises enables the Church to provide some Catholic instruction to Catholic children who out of choice or necessity remain in the public school system, while at the same time avoiding the danger of Protestant proselytization and instruction. The Catholic Church was never opposed to the released-time plan; its previous non-co-operation was based entirely on the belief that the results obtainable under it did not warrant the effort required to sustain it. The present Catholic change of position, therefore, might well be explained simply as the result of a re-evaluation of the ratio between the results and the effort required to achieve them.

So simple an explanation is not available for the energy, if not passion, with which the Catholic Church now espouses programs for the introduction of religious teachings and exercises within the public schools. At first glance, this new approach not only disregards long-standing Catholic fears of Protestant proselytization but seems to run counter to the dictates of Catholic religious dogma. Take, for example, the so-called "common core" proposal. This is based on the assumption that the three major faiths have certain basic common beliefs (e.g., belief in God, the Ten Commandments, the efficacy of prayer, etc.) which can and should be taught the children in the public schools. Naturally, this was initially a Protestant idea, for it is merely an extension of the pan-Protestantism that arose when Protestant dissent swallowed the established churches. But such an approach seems to run dangerously counter to the spirit of Catholic dogma, for it seems to imply the equality of faiths and to deny the exclusiveness of Catholic truth.

Nevertheless, after the Zorach decision, representatives of the Protestant Council of New York, the Roman Catholic Archdiocese, and the New York Board of Rabbis (the latter with extreme reluctance) for months attempted jointly to work out an acceptable "common core" program for use in the New York City public schools. The endeavor finally came to an end when the Board of Rabbis decided to inform the Protestant and Catholic representatives and the city Board of Education that agreement on a program was impossible and that no useful purpose would be served by continuing the effort to arrive at agreement. In Indianapolis, on the other hand, a "common core" program based on the Ten Commandments was agreed upon by a Protestant minister, a Catholic priest, and a rabbi (here, too, the latter with extreme reluctance), but was not introduced into the public schools because the attorney for the Board of Education advised the board that it violated the Constitution.

Catholic support for programs to teach "moral and spiritual values" in the public schools is likewise at variance with the previous Catholic opposition to religion in the public schools. The term "moral and spiritual values" has been in use at least since 1944 and was probably coined by Professor William C. Bower of the University of Chicago. It became popular after 1951 with the publication of a report, entitled *Moral and Spiritual Values in the Public Schools*, by the Educational Policies Commission of the National Educational

Association. The report grew out of increasingly articulate criticism of the public schools for neglecting religion. The report consists of some one hundred printed pages, almost all devoted to moral, ethical, and civic values. Some seven or eight pages are devoted to the subject of religion. In substance these say that the public schools should be friendly toward religion; should guard religious freedom and tolerance; can and should teach about religion in an objective way without indoctrination; should not compel teachers to affiliate or not affiliate with any religious group nor impose any religious test for appointment in the public schools; and should not permit the reading of the Bible or even the Old Testament, since it must be recognized that our schools serve many who claim no religious affiliations or convictions whatever.

The popularity of the term "moral and spiritual values" is probably best explained by the fact that it is not easily defined and therefore can mean all things to all men. It has gained special favor with public school administrators faced with charges that the schools are "Godless." Groups seeking to inject religious education into the school system have fastened onto the phrase as a useful and attractive device to achieve their goal. Foremost among these have been spokesmen for the Catholic Church. When a proposal to introduce a program for teaching moral and spiritual values was considered in New York City in 1956, Catholic groups were its most articulate and vigorous supporters, criticizing it only because it did not go far enough in equating the moral and spiritual with the religious or in providing for outright religious instruction.

Catholic demands for the intensification of the religious content of Christmas and Easter programs in the public schools—strongly opposed by the Jewish groups—and for the erection of crosses, crèches, and other Christological symbols on public school and other municipal premises are understandable and less inconsistent with the previous position of the Church. But Catholic groups also support the placing of the Ten Commandments on the walls of public school classrooms, even though Catholic numbering and text of the commandments differ from the Protestant and Jewish versions. And Catholic priests are now willing to co-operate with Protestant ministers and with rabbis in culling selections from the Bible that would be acceptable to all three faiths for reading in the public schools.

In short, I think it is a fair estimate of the situation to say that whereas for a century the Catholic Church and the Catholic community in America were strongly opposed to religious instruction or exercises in the public schools, they have now become their most articulate and ardent champions. I think also that the explanation for this complete reversal in position lies in the fact that Catholicism has passed from the defensive and has become an active and confident protagonist in American cultural competition, and as such has recognized the tremendous potential of public school religious education in the competition.

Whereas the Catholic groups favor religion in the public schools, the Jewish groups oppose it. While a rabbi or a board of rabbis will occasionally sit down with Catholic and Protestant representatives in an attempt to work out a mutually acceptable common-core or moral and spiritual values program, it is hardly a secret that they are not motivated by a belief in the desirability of their efforts but by a feeling that they cannot say no. The Jewish community too, however, is passing from the defensive and more and more rabbis and rabbinical boards do say no. The program for the teaching of moral and spiritual values in the public schools of New York City vigorously supported by the representatives of Catholic organizations was opposed with equal vigor by the New York Board of Rabbis. There is hardly a Jewish organization in the nation, rabbinic or congregational, that does not oppose religious instruction or exercises in the public schools.

The unanimity in Catholicism and in Judaism (on opposite sides) is not matched by a similar unanimity in Protestantism. There is within Protestantism a segment that would remain true to the libertarianism of Protestant dissent. In Virginia the state Baptist conference in 1958 protested Bible instruction in the schools and went so far as to threaten legal action to discontinue it. *Church and State*, the publication of Protestants and Other Americans United for Separation of Church and State, frequently expresses opposition to the released-time program. Unitarians, Christian Scientists, and other Protestant sects often express similar views. But these probably represent a minority within Protestantism. The National Council of Churches favors the released-time program, although it recommends that the restrictions imposed by the McCollum decision should be adhered to. Increasingly within Protestantism we hear echoes of Catholic charges of the Godlessness of public education and demands that through instruction in moral and spiritual values or otherwise the public schools undertake greater responsibility for religious education.

The group within Protestantism that represents the original dissent lays principal emphasis on the separation of church and state. Its members would forego the temptation to use the public school as an aid to promoting religious education so as not to compromise the principle of separation. They recognize the basic inconsistency of attacking Roman Catholic infringements on this principle while at the same time supporting and promoting public school involvement in religious education. The second group, which probably by now represents the major part of organized Protestantism, lays greater emphasis on the need to advance religious education and the role that the public school can play in furthering this objective. To the cry of the "separationists" within Protestantism that the "educationalists" are playing "the Catholics' game," the latter reply that the "separationists" are playing the secularists' game. The "separationists" consider the Roman Catholic Church as the greatest threat to Protestant cultural values; the "educationalists" view secularism and irreligion as the greatest menace.

The "educationalists" within Protestantism appear willing to join in a new alliance with Catholicism to reintroduce some religious education into the public schools. (New York City's proposal for instruction in moral and spiritual values was supported by the Protestant Council of New York, even if with somewhat less enthusiasm than that of the Catholic spokesmen.) The "educationalists" are probably not yet prepared to enter into a grand alliance that would encompass endorsement of the narrow interpretation of the First Amendment. This would require acceptance of governmental aid to parochial schools, and no significant element within Protestantism is yet ready for that. A major part of Protestantism, however, appears to indicate willingness to accept the lesser alliance—limited to religion in the public schools—which Catholicism today eagerly offers. Whether Protestantism can long continue thus to enjoy the best of both possible worlds—the exclusion of parochial schools from governmental aid and the inclusion of pan-Protestantism in the public schools—or will inevitably be forced into the grand alliance which is the ultimate objective of the Catholic Church, is a question that only time can answer.

5. PRIVATE SCHOOLS AND THE PUBLIC PURSE

THE CATHOLIC PAROCHIAL SCHOOL

It is not beyond the realm of possibility that had the Catholic child in the nineteenth century received the same cordial welcome from the public school given the Jewish child in the twentieth, and that had the religious conscience of the Catholic child been respected as was the Jewish child's, the Catholic community might have adjusted to the American public school system. It might not have expended so large a portion of its worldly goods and income in establishing and maintaining a gigantic separate and parallel school system. To accomplish this it would have had to defy the urgent insistence of the Church, and whether it would have done so must remain in the realm of speculation. What can be said without speculation is that the treatment accorded to Catholic children in the pan-Protestant public schools of the mid-nineteenth century was not such as to encourage Catholic parents to counter the demands of the Church. The beatings and expulsions suffered by Catholic children who refused to participate in Protestant Bible reading or exercises made inevitable what might not otherwise have occurred.

Undoubtedly the Catholic Church would have striven for the establishment of a separate Catholic school system irrespective of the treatment accorded Catholic children in the public schools. Justice Jackson, in his dissenting opinion in the Everson parochial school bus case, noted that "the parochial school is a vital, if not the most vital, part of the Roman Catholic Church." He expressed the opinion that if put to the choice, the Church "would forego its whole service for mature persons before it would give up education of the young";

that "its growth and cohesion, discipline and loyalty, spring from its schools," and that "Catholic education is the rock on which the whole structure rests."

The adjustment, accepted reluctantly by Protestantism and gladly by Judaism, of combining secular education in a public school with religious education in a Sunday or after-hour religious school would not have been acceptable to the Catholic Church. The primary reason is not that the Church would consider inadequate the amount of religious education obtainable on Sundays or after regular school hours on weekdays. What is unacceptable to the Church is the basic premise of the American public school system, as accorded constitutional sanction in the Everson, McCollum, and Zorach cases. That premise is (again quoting Justice Jackson) "that secular education can be isolated from all religious teaching so that the school can inculcate all needed temporal knowledge and also maintain a strict and lofty neutrality in religion."

Secular education isolated from religious teaching is a concept completely unacceptable in Catholic dogma. As stated by Pius XI in his encyclical "On the Christian Education of Youth," "there can be no true education which is not wholly directed to man's last end. . . . From this it follows, that the so-called 'neutral' or 'lay' school, from which religion is excluded, is contrary to the fundamental principles of education." Moreover, even if such a school gives some religious instruction along with its regular secular curriculum, that fact, the encyclical continues, "does not bring it into accord with the rights of the Church and of the Christian family, or make it a fit place for Catholic students. To be this it is necessary that all the teaching and the whole organization of the school, and its teachers, syllabus and textbooks in every branch, be regulated by the Christian spirit, under the direction and material supervision of the Church."

It is thus obvious that whatever might have been the evolution of the public educational system, the Church would have striven for its own school system to achieve the goal, stated in the encyclical, of "Catholic education in Catholic schools for all the Catholic youth." Through the combined efforts of the Catholic Church and the Catholic community, a vast parochial system has been established and is maintained all over the nation. But a little less than four million children attend Catholic elementary schools, and more than three quarters of a million attend Catholic high schools. The rate of growth can be appreciated by comparing this combined figure of

4,700,000 given in *The Official Catholic Directory* for 1958 with the figure of about 3,335,000 given by the same source for 1952. In other words, in a period of six years there has been according to the same official Catholic source an increase of approximately 40 per cent in enrollment in Catholic elementary and secondary schools. In 1952, Francis M. Crowley, dean of the School of Education of Fordham University, estimated that the "Catholic Church cares for approximately sixty per cent of all Catholic children in parochial schools." There is no reason to believe that this percentage will not increase and the growth of Catholic parochial education will not continue. Nor is there any reason to doubt the validity of Justice Jackson's opinion that the parochial school may well be the most vital part of the Roman Catholic Church.

NON–CATHOLIC PRIVATE SCHOOLS

Parochial schools among Protestants are scarce. Even if one includes church-related schools it is doubtful that the total of children attending Protestant private elementary and secondary schools equals one-tenth the number attending Catholic parochial schools. Nor is there any evidence that the percentage of children attending Protestant schools is increasing to any appreciable extent. The majority of Protestant parochial schools are conducted by Lutherans. Proportionate to the total number of children of elementary and secondary school age in each denomination, however, the Seventh Day Adventists are probably first; it may well be that the percentage of Seventh Day Adventist children attending the parochial schools of that denomination is higher than the percentage of Catholic children of school age attending Catholic parochial schools, although the number itself is very small.

It cannot be denied that despite the commitment of American Jewry to public education there has recently been a trend within the Jewish community away from the public schools and to private schools. This trend, though at present not large, is far from insignificant. Several factors contribute toward it. In the first place, the Jewish community, like all other segments of the American community, is affected by the current wave of religiosity that appears to be sweeping the country. Education being so substantial an element in Judaism, it is natural that this return to religion should be reflected in an intensification of religious training. This in turn results in an increase in Jewish parochial or day schools in which a more complete religious training can be impaired than is available in the Jewish after-hour or Sunday schools.

The second cause is the rapid economic rise of American Jewry. American Jews are now largely a middle-class group with a generous percentage in upper income brackets. Like their Gentile neighbors of equivalent economic standing, they can afford to provide their children with schooling superior to that available in overcrowded and understaffed public school classrooms. The modern Jewish day school is, by and large, a progressive school with small classes and enriched curricula. A substantial percentage of the pupils attending are children of parents whose motivation in sending them there is not at all religious.

A third factor in the trend appears to be the fear on the part of some Jewish parents of the increasingly articulate and intensive demands to desecularize the public schools. To these parents desecularization can mean only Christianization, and they feel that if their children must receive religious education along with the secular schooling, they would prefer the religious education to be that of their own faith.

Finally, a significant if not always expressed factor is the instinct toward cultural and religious survival and the fear of assimilation and the disappearance of Judaism and Jewry in an environment where the cohesive pressures of anti-Semitism are absent.

Besides the Protestant and Jewish private schools, there are of course secular private schools and academies on the elementary and secondary school levels. These are attended almost exclusively by children of parents in the high income brackets and therefore constitute an almost negligible element in the American educational system.

All in all, non-Catholic private education in the United States is of relatively small importance. The *National Catholic Almanac* estimated in 1955 that 94 per cent of children in non-public elementary schools and 83 per cent of children in non-public high schools attend Catholic schools. It is quite obvious that the problems raised by private education are the problems raised by Catholic parochial schools and that the attack on and defense of private education is for all practical purposes an attack on and defense of Catholic parochial education.

CONS AND PROS OF PAROCHIAL EDUCATION

Catholic criticism of public education has been matched by non-Catholic criticism of parochial education. The indictment against the parochial school has many counts. Perhaps most frequently heard is the charge that the system is divisive in effect and probably in intent as well. It is the most prominent instance of Catholic separatism. It creates a cultural ghetto in which Catholic children are isolated and insulated from their fellow Americans.

Jefferson once expressed the view that "by bringing the sects together, and mixing them with the mass of other students, we shall soften their asperities, liberalize and neutralize their prejudices and make the general religion a religion of peace, reason, and morality." The National Education Association, in 1955, made the same point:

The American child who attends the public school has learned, played and grown up with children of many different religious faiths and ethnic groups. In the give and take of growing up together, public school children have learned the real meaning of brotherhood; they have become friends with children of all faiths. Only a common school can serve this great end.

The parochial school does just the opposite and does it during the school years when human beings are most impressionable and when the patterns for adult living are shaped. James Bryant Conant said, "The greater the proportion of our youth who fail to attend our public schools and who receive their education elsewhere, the greater the threat to our democratic unity."

A second count in the indictment of parochial school education lies in the nature of the education. Roman Catholicism is authoritarian in spirit and discipline and the education imparted in its schools must necessarily be authoritarian. Respect for authority, a cardinal virtue in Catholic education, is more in the nature of a necessary evil in a democracy born out of a revolt against authority, whose major holiday commemorates a declaration of independence of authority and whose legitimacy is predicated upon an inalienable right of self-government which is superior to authority.

Moreover, Catholic culture is corporative and collective, and the education imparted in Catholic schools aims at a perpetuation and expansion of such a culture. American culture produced by the alliance of Protestant dissent and secular humanism is individualistic. One frequently hears from Catholic sources attacks upon statism and the cry that the state is made for man and not man for the state. Non-Catholic Americans committed to the democratic concepts evolved out of the Protestant-humanist alliance vigorously agree with this but extend it further and urge with equal vigor that the church is made for man and not man for the church. Roman Catholicism, it is charged, is not willing to accept this extension and the nature of the training received by Catholic children in Catholic schools reflects that refusal.

Other charges are perhaps less important. The secular education received in Catholic parochial schools, it is argued, is generally inferior to that available in public schools. The reason is that the educational equipment, personnel, and standards are below those in the public schools. The classes are overcrowded, more overcrowded than public school classes. Most of the teaching personnel are nuns, many of whom lack the pedagogical training required of licensed public school teachers and all of whom have renounced the world in which the children they are training will live. Pedagogical methods employed are frequently old-fashioned and outdated. The hours in parochial schools are substantially the same as those in public schools, but in the former a large portion of the time is devoted to religious instruction with the result that secular instruction must inevitably suffer. While parochial schools are subject to state inspection and are required to meet certain minimum standards, inspection is often little more than perfunctory if it is conducted at all.

The defenders of the Catholic educational system are particularly bitter about criticism based upon the physical inadequacy of the parochial schools. Such criticism does not come with good grace from those who vigorously oppose any effort to improve the situation through public funds. Those who send their children to parochial schools because their conscience so dictates are not thereby relieved of any part of their obligation as taxpayers to support the public schools. They must in addition sustain a vast educational system solely out of voluntary efforts. With such uneven terms of competition it is surprising that the gap between the facilities and personnel of parochial and public schools is not far wider than it is. Furthermore, despite all the difficulties and hardships, the gap is steadily closing. New parochial schools constantly being built are far superior to many of the existing public schools in physical facilities and equal to the new public schools being erected at a much smaller proportionate rate. Lay teachers, having the same qualifications as teachers in the public schools and receiving substantially the same salaries, are being employed in parochial schools in increasing numbers.

Catholics gladly admit that great emphasis is placed on respect for authority in parochial education. They assert that the rising tide of juvenile delinquency and the low moral and ethical standards of the adult generation are to a large extent attributable to the fact that the public schools have neglected adequately to teach respect for authority. The choice is between lawlessness and authority, and the Catholics proudly prefer authority.

Similarly, Catholics do not apologize for the large proportion of time devoted to religious instruction in the parochial school day. Logically, religion is either the most important thing in life or it is nothing at all, and to Catholics it is the former. Religion in Catholic philosophy is the end of life, secular pursuits are the means; to impair religious education in favor of secular instruction is therefore to compromise the end in favor of the means. The purpose of Catholic living is to gain eternal salvation and to avoid eternal damnation; it is both wrong and foolish to compromise that purpose simply to gain a few additional hours of secular instruction which can be of no use or value after we have lived the minute period of time allotted us on this earth.

Catholics are not prepared to concede that parochial education is any more divisive than public education. In the first place, it is an unproved assumption that living together and knowing each other necessarily leads to brotherhood and fellowship; the experience of Negro-white relationships in the South attests to that. In the second place, there is in many respects a greater diversity in parochial schools than in public schools. The intentional or *de facto* zoning which divides neighborhoods into upper class and lower class, Negro and white, Puerto Rican and native in the East, Mexican and native in the Southwest, results in public schools that are largely homogeneous in economic, social, and ethnic groupings. Such homogeneity, if not completely absent in parochial schools, is far less prominent. If the children in parochial schools are all of one religion, they are more likely to be of different social, economic, racial, and ethnic origins.

Actually, the major defense of the parochial school lies in the concept of cultural pluralism. There was a time, particularly after World War I, when nationalism was at its height and cultural uniformity a greatly desired end. It was the era that was committed to the melting-pot theory whereby persons of different nationalities and cultures were all miraculously (for obviously God so willed it) transformed into the American pattern. It was the era which (not to strain God's powers unduly) enacted an immigration law and policy designed to insure that the overwhelming majority of those who came to settle here were already in substantial measure just like us (i.e., Aryan or Nordic) so that the process of acculturalization, assimilation, and Americanization would be quick and relatively painless. It was an era that frowned upon the study of foreign languages in the schools, looked with contempt upon "hyphenated Americans," and generally eschewed all that was foreign and strange.

The nation has happily outgrown this adolescent stage in its development. Americans now recognize, or at least are beginning to recognize, that unity and uniformity are not synonymous; that unity may lie in diversity; that we are a nation not only of people but of peoples; that American culture is a plurality of cultures. If we recognize that diversity is a good to be sought and not an evil to be eradicated, we must recognize that a plurality of educational systems is likewise a good to be preserved. When we recognize the powerful uniformity-producing capacities of the mass communication media— television, radio, cinema, *Life*, *Look* and *The Saturday Evening Post* —we should be grateful for the existence of a school system that helps provide a welcome change from the even more powerful uniformity-producing public school education.

PRIVATE SCHOOLS AND THE LAW

If, as seems reasonable, the preservation and perpetuation of private and parochial schools are indispensable to the preservation of a pluralistic society, then those committed to a pluralistic America owe a great debt to the Catholic Church, just as those committed to a secular public school system owe it a great debt. The contribution of the Church to cultural pluralism is not limited to the maintenance of an independent school system inculcating a culture somewhat different from what is viewed as traditional American culture, but includes a major responsibility for developing in our law the principle that cultural pluralism is constitutionally protected.

The first step in this development occurred in 1923 and involved Lutheran rather than Catholic parochial schools. The xenophobia that accompanied World War I and the period immediately following it gave rise to the enactment in several Western and Midwestern states of laws prohibiting the teaching of foreign languages in public or private schools at the elementary level. A number of teachers in Lutheran schools in Ohio, Nebraska, and Iowa were prosecuted for violating these laws by teaching the German language to children in the schools. In *Meyer* v. *Nebraska*, the United States Supreme Court, to which the teachers appealed, threw out the convictions and held the laws unconstitutional. There was nothing evil or dangerous to the welfare of the community, the Court held, in children learning a foreign language. If lingual (and hence cultural) uniformity is desirable it must be sought through voluntary means and not through compulsion.

Two years later the Court followed the Meyer decision in the case of *Pierce* v. *Society of Sisters*, the famous Oregon parochial school case. Here what was involved was not merely a law prohibiting the teaching of foreign languages in private or parochial schools but one which in effect outlawed such schools altogether by requiring that all children attend public schools. The decision of the United States Supreme Court invalidating the Oregon statute may well be called the Magna Carta of private schools in America and perhaps as well the Magna Carta of cultural pluralism. In this decision the Court ruled that under our system of constitutionally guaranteed liberties the government may not outlaw private schools and thus confer upon the public schools a monopoly in the shaping and transmission of cultural patterns and values. "The fundamental theory of liberty upon which all governments in this Union repose," said the Court, "excludes any general power of the State to standardize its children by forcing them to accept instruction from public teachers only."

The parents who sent their children to the Oregon parochial schools did so because their religious conscience as Catholics compelled them to, and the Oregon law proscribing parochial schools thus infringed upon religious liberty. But the Court's decision went beyond protecting church schools; it encompassed all private schools. It protected not merely religious liberty but cultural pluralism, not merely those whose motivation was religious but all who did not wish their children to be standardized according to the public school standard. The same decision that spread the mantle of constitutional protection around the Catholic parochial school held that a parent who wished to send his child to a private military academy instead of a public school could not constitutionally be restrained from doing so. And, two years after the Pierce case, the Court, following that decision and the Meyer decision, held that a bilingual (Japanese-American) school was similarly protected from unreasonable governmental restraint or harassment.

These decisions did not outlaw cultural uniformity as a desirable governmental objective; they did no more than outlaw compulsion as a means of achieving that objective. The fact that a state could not compel all children to attend public rather than private or parochial schools does not preclude the state from attempting to make the public schools so attractive through expansion of their facilities and elevating their pedagogic standards that parents would willingly send their children there rather than to non-public schools. Nor do these decisions immunize private and parochial schools from governmental inspection to assure their adherence to minimum standards of secular education. The states may and do require that children attending non-public schools receive instruction in such basic secular subjects as English language and writing, reading, arithmetic and history. The states may also require, although not all do, that the teachers in the non-public schools imparting this secular instruction establish their qualifications through obtaining officially issued licenses.

Actually, the state laws for inspection and supervision of private and parochial schools are honored more often in the breach than in the observance. For a variety of reasons, inspection and supervision are generally either perfunctory or entirely absent. Except in the most extreme cases, state education officials do not act against even egregiously substandard parochial schools.

What effectively keeps the Catholic Church authorities diligent in maintaining and improving facilities, equipment, and pedagogic standards in the parochial schools is not the visiting power of state officials, but the competition of the public schools. Unless the parochial schools are substantially equal to the public schools in plant, curriculum, and teaching methods, a great many Catholic parents will refuse to send their children there, no matter how insistent may be the urging of the priests. Because the Church realizes this and because it realizes further that the parochial schools system constitutes its major asset in the competition of cultures and that without that system it might just as well close up shop, the Church strives mightily not merely to expand the system but continually to improve it and keep it at least as attractive as the public school system.

This requires a tremendous amount of money, more money than the Catholic community can easily afford to pay. And as the parochial school program expands, ever-increasing amounts of money will be required, particularly as the source of unpaid nun teachers becomes exhausted and must be supplemented in large numbers by lay teachers who must be paid salaries more or less equivalent to those paid in the public schools. As the financial burden on the Catholic community increases, so too do the intensity and urgency of Catholic demands for a share of the tax-raised funds to support their parochial schools. What the ultimate outcome will be cannot be predicted; but one thing is certain: the Catholic community cannot indefinitely carry alone the financial burden of the school system which the Church deems indispensable for the fulfillment of its mission and the maintenance of its position in the competition of cultures.

PUBLIC FUNDS FOR PAROCHIAL SCHOOLS?—THE CATHOLICS' CASE

Undoubtedly the controversy on public funds for parochial schools is the single most serious factor for interreligious disharmony and friction between Protestantism and Catholicism. As in the dispute on Amerircan diplomatic representation at the Vatican there is a practical unanimity on each side of the issue. But while Catholics generally consider the exchange of ambassadors with the Vatican a relatively unimportant matter not worth the acrimony it engenders, they view the question of public funds for parochial schools in an entirely different light. This to them is not merely an important matter, it is a vital one, for the growth and perhaps even the continued existence of the parochial school system probably depends upon the availability of tax-raised funds for its support.

The difficulty, if not impossibility, of finding a solution to the problem satisfactory to both Catholics and Protestants rests upon the diametrically opposite views taken by the two faiths of the position of the parochial school in the American educational system. The Catholics view it as an integral and desirable part of that system, the Protestants as at best a necessary evil—evil for the reasons stated earlier in the chapter, and necessary because the Supreme Court has ruled that it cannot constitutionally be destroyed. We will defer for a moment discussion of the Protestant position and consider now the Catholic case for allowing parochial schools to share tax-raised funds.

Catholic philosophy of government does not recognize education as a function of the state. Education is the exclusive right and responsibility of the parent. When the state enters into the field of education it acts solely as the agent of the parents. Except in a narrow field of specialized education, such as military training and training for government service, the state has nothing to teach. We recognize that today the state has undertaken another responsibility, that of compelling all parents to supply their children with a minimum of basic education. While this responsibility does not seem consistent with the true role of the democratic state as the servant rather than the master of the parents, it has become universally accepted as a legitimate function of a democratic state. But, as the Supreme Court held in the Oregon case, the parents have the right to furnish their children with this minimum secular education in public, private, or parochial schools, as their taste and conscience dictate. The democratic state cannot compel them to supply it exclusively through public schools since that would make the state the master and not the servant of the parents.

With the accepted power of the state to require all parents to supply their children with a minimum education came the incidental power to inspect all schools to ascertain whether they do in fact provide that education. But with it also comes a concomitant duty, the duty of enabling the parents to supply that education. Unless poverty can legitimately be declared to be a crime, the state cannot legally or morally compel a parent to provide an education for his children and then punish him for not having the financial means to provide that education. Hence, the state, or more accurately the local community, provides free public schools which the parents may patronize in discharge of their obligations under the compulsory education laws.

But some parents—specifically Catholic parents—violate their conscience by sending their children to common schools or schools where they do not receive Catholic religious training along with secular education. These parents, as we have seen, cannot directly be coerced into going against their scruples by punishing them for not sending their children to common schools. Yet, if they lack the financial resources to pay the tuition necessary to maintain parochial schools and thus are unable to send their children to parochial schools, they are indirectly but with equal effectiveness coerced into sending their children to public schools and thus repudiating their principles. In a democracy, freedom of conscience should not be a privilege available exclusively to the well-to-do.

The only fair solution is for the state to make it possible for Catholic parents to comply with the requirements of the compulsory education law without violating the dictates of their conscience and to comply with their principles without transgressing the compulsory education law. The state can practicably accomplish this in any one of a variety of ways. It can make grants of money to parents who elect to send their children to parochial schools. It can allow parochial schools directly to share in tax-raised funds. Or it can adopt the system in effect in the province of Quebec where separate Catholic and Protestant school systems operate and every taxpayer, upon paying his tax for education, specifies to which system he wishes the payment to go. The particular method employed is not important; what is important is to recognize the injustice and basically undemocratic nature of the present monopoly of public school education in public funds.

Of course, inclusion of parochial schools in a governmental program for financing education constitutes a recognition that such schools are part of the state's educational system. But this recognition was implicit if not explicit in the Supreme Court's decision in the Oregon case. There is nothing incongruous in having a nation's educational system composed of both public and private schools equal in status and equal in respect to governmental financing. Such a system prevails in the Netherlands, and there is no reason why it should not prevail here.

Nor do Catholics find any difficulty in respect to the constitutional guaranty of separation of church and state. If the funds are paid not to the parochial schools but to the parents, then the aid is to them and not to the church, and there is therefore no grant of public funds to religious bodies. Even if the funds are paid to the church schools, Catholics find no violation of the First Amendment, for they interpret that amendment to bar only preferential aid to religion and the program they urge encompasses all church schools without discrimination or preference.

PROTESTANT OPPOSITION

As united as are Catholics in their claim to a share in public funds for their parochial schools so Protestants are united in their opposition to that claim. Many grounds are asserted by Protestants for their opposition, but by far most often and most vigorously heard is the cry that a grant of tax-raised funds to parochial schools would violate the principle of separation of church and state. To many Protestants separation of church and state means little more than the exclusion of churches and church schools from any program for the expenditure of tax-raised funds.

Concentration of Protestant concern on this one aspect of church-state relations has led some Catholics to suggest that what makes the Protestants cry out is not that they like separation more but that they like the Catholic Church less. Yet there is much to explain this concentration completely independent of Protestant feeling toward Catholicism. Taxation for religious purposes was the principal battlefield in the revolution of Protestant dissent against established Protestantism in America. As the Supreme Court noted in the Everson case, the "imposition of taxes to pay ministers' salaries and to build and maintain churches and church property aroused the indignation" of freedom-loving colonials long before anyone conceived of Catholic churches and Catholic institutions as possible beneficiaries of such taxes. At the time of the Revolutionary War almost every colony exacted some kind of tax for church support. In New England many dissenting Protestants were jailed for refusing to pay the tax levied to support the established Congregational Church. In Virginia, Patrick Henry soared overnight to fame and embarked on his brilliant career because of his speech in "The Parson's Case," which crystallized the common people's resistance to taxation for church purposes. In Virginia, too, resistance by Protestant dissent to taxation for church purposes resulted in the disestablishment of the Anglican Church and in Jefferson's monumental Statute Establishing Religious Freedom. It is not too much to suggest that the tradition of

Protestant dissent is largely a tradition of resistance to taxation for church purposes. One need not, therefore, look at Protestant un-friendliness to Catholicism for an explanation for Protestant identi-fication of separation of church and state with the non-expenditure of tax-raised funds for churches or church schools.

Yet it remains true that a substantial part of Protestant opposition to public funds for parochial schools is predicated upon its opposi-tion to the parochial schools themselves. As we have seen, Protestants generally look at the Catholic parochial school system as at best a necessary evil and they are not likely to favor extension or even perpetuation of the system at public expense. They consider paro-chial schools a threat to the unity of public education and to allow them to share in funds raised by taxation for public education would be to require the public education system to finance its own dissolu-tion. They look with horror at the experience of the Netherlands, often pointed to by Catholics as a model to be followed, where the institution of a system of state subsidies to confessional schools re-sulted in the withdrawal of four out of every five schools from the public education system to private operation and control. Protestants would consider it a disaster if the American common school system were to be fragmentized into a host of rival sectarian systems all fighting for more money from the public treasury and dividing the community into narrow-minded segments.

Protestants have no sympathy for the claim of the Catholics that they are being unfairly subjected to double taxation. This claim is based upon an assumption that Protestants reject, namely, that edu-cation is a commodity benefiting only the child receiving it and that therefore the parent should be free to purchase that commodity either from a public or a private vendor as his tastes dictate. To Protestants the education of children benefits all of society and not merely the children receiving the education. Were this not so, there would be no moral justification for imposing school taxes upon the childless and upon those whose children have passed school age.

THE JEWISH POSITION

While the Jews do not feel as strongly on the question as the Protestants, their position is much the same and is held with much the same unanimity. They agree that public subsidies to religious schools would violate the constitutional principle of the separation of church and state to which they are strongly committed. For that reason they refrain from seeking tax-raised funds for their own religious schools and cheerfully undertake to support these schools through their own voluntary contributions. While there are some Jewish religious leaders, particularly in Reform or Liberal Judaism, that agree with Protestants in viewing parochial schools with disfavor, the rapid growth of Jewish religious day schools is evidence that probably most rabbis do not share this view. They do, however, agree that desirable as Jewish religious schools are, they should not be financed out of the public treasury.

INDIRECT AID AND THE EVERSON CASE

The constitutions and laws in all the states of the Union prohibit the states from making direct grants of public funds to church schools or for religious education. The Constitution of the United States, as interpreted by the Supreme Court, contains the same prohibition. In the 1952 Zorach case, the latest opinion on the question expressed by the Court, it was specifically stated that under the First and Fourteenth Amendments to the Constitution "government may not finance religious groups." It is the Catholic position that this is an incorrect interpretation of what the framers of the First and Fourteenth Amendments intended and that the constitutional principle of separation of church and state, correctly interpreted, does not bar government from financing religious groups or religious education so long as it does so on a non-preferential basis. Nevertheless, the Constitution is what the Supreme Court says it is, and it does not appear likely that the Court will radically alter its interpretation in the near future.

While the Constitution bars the states from directly financing religious education or church schools, it does allow what has become known as indirect aid to such schools. In the case of *Cochran* v. *Louisiana State Board of Education*, the Supreme Court held in 1930 that a state could constitutionally expend public funds for the purchase of secular textbooks to be furnished without charge for use by children attending parochial schools. The purpose of the expenditure, the Court said, was to aid the children; that the church schools were indirectly aided by the fact that if the state did not provide the books they would have to, did not render the expenditure unconstitutional.

The Cochran decision aroused little excitement, but the Everson decision, handed down in 1947 by a Court split five to four, aroused a storm of controversy and led directly to the formation of the organization, Protestants and Other Americans United for Separation of Church and State. In the Everson case the Court ruled that a state could constitutionally expend public funds to transport children by bus to parochial schools. The decision followed logically from the decision in the Cochran case, although the majority of the Court used a somewhat different approach in reaching it. The Court did not speak in terms of direct or indirect aid, but construed the purpose of the expenditure to be to protect children from traffic hazards, holding that what was challenged was not aid to religious education but a child-welfare benefit.

If constitutionality is dependent upon whether the state aid is to welfare or education, there would seem to be a narrower area of allowable aid than if the test is whether the church school is the direct or indirect beneficiary. If the former test is used, it appears that use of public funds for the purchase of secular textbooks to be used in church schools would be unconstitutional. Yet American Protestantism accepted the Cochran decision with no substantial protest but was aroused to great passion and to organize for the defense of separation of church and state by the Everson decision.

The explanation, I think, lies in the difference in the position of American Catholicism in 1930 and in 1947. In 1930 Catholics still appeared to be a submerged minority subject to bigotry and discrimination. The fact that a Catholic had been nominated for the Presidency by one of the nation's two major parties really marked the end of the period during which anti-Catholic bigotry was a substantial factor in American life. But this was not widely recognized at the time. What was more apparent and more dramatic was the fact that the Catholic candidate had been decisively beaten and that there had been considerable expression of anti-Catholic bigotry during the course of the campaign, particularly in the South. Parochial schools, limited largely to a few major metropolitan areas and serving only a small minority of Catholic children, did not threaten the monopoly of the common school in the nation's educational system, and Catholicism itself constituted no apparent threat to the Protestant-humanist monopoly of American culture.

By 1947 the situation had changed. Catholicism was no longer on the defensive. It had emerged as a real competitor in the market of culture, a competitor to be reckoned with. Although the statement may be an oversimplification, I think it basically true that in 1930 American Protestantism was motivated by sympathy for Catholics, whereas in 1947 it was motivated by fear of the Catholic Church and Catholic culture concepts and values. By 1947 the Catholic Church had launched its campaign to expand the parochial school system. By 1947 the parochial school had become a real competitor of the public school and all indications pointed to its steady expansion and growing importance.

Therein, I suggest, lies the explanation for Protestant opposition to use of public funds for bus transportation to parochial schools and its suspicion of the use of public funds to supply hot lunches or medical and dental care to children attending parochial schools. Protestants do not want Catholic children to suffer the hazards of traffic or the hardships of inclement weather while going to school. Nor do they begrudge them hot lunches or medical and dental care at public expense. What they fear is the "opening wedge." They suspect that the Church is exploiting the needs of children and the sympathy for children to promote its own ends. They are apprehensive that the Church will not be content with the extension of public lunch and medical programs to children in parochial schools, or even the extension of public bus transportation to parochial schools, but will simply regard them as steps toward the ultimate goal of making the parochial school an equal partner with the public school in the nation's educational system. Because Protestants so strongly oppose the last step, they find it difficult to accept measures that may be the first, however just and humane those measures would appear to be in themselves.

6. MORALS, CENSORSHIP, AND BLUE SUNDAY

OUR CHANGING MORALS

Early in 1957 the Lord's Day Alliance of the United States held its sixty-eighth annual convention and listened to its general secretary, the Rev. Dr. Melvin M. Forney, deliver an eloquent address announcing a nation-wide campaign to enact stringent laws against the liquor trade, gambling, and violations of the Sabbath. There was nothing particularly unique about this speech; undoubtedly much the same sort of address had been delivered at previous annual conventions of the Alliance by Dr. Forney's predecessors since 1889. What was noteworthy and a little pathetic about the speech was that it was being delivered in 1957.

It was an address declaiming against the liquor traffic at a time when gigantic electric signs advertised a myriad of brands of liquors, when every newspaper carried similar advertisements, when beer advertisements were brought into every home through brewery-sponsored telecasts of popular sporting events. It declaimed against gambling at a time when state after state was legalizing bingo; when betting on horse racing had been legalized practically everywhere and newspapers regularly carried the betting odds not only on horse racing but on professional baseball, football, basketball, and a host of other sports. And it declaimed against Sabbath-breaking at a time when Sunday was the most profitable day for all forms of professional entertainments and sports and was rapidly becoming a profitable day for retail trade.

What was pathetic was that both the speaker and his audience appeared totally unaware of the radical change that had taken place, and was continuing to take place, in our nation's moral standards. For more than two centuries the nation's moral standards and the penal codes embodying those standards had been dictated by Calvinist Protestantism. With the second quarter of the twentieth century came a new challenge to the Calvinist monopoly, hitherto opposed—and rather ineffectively—only by secularism. The new challenge came from Roman Catholicism which had just established itself as a potent protagonist in the competition of cultures. It is more than a coincidence that the Eighteenth Amendment, the last great effort of Calvinist Protestantism to assert its dominance of the nation's moral code, was repealed but a few years after a Roman Catholic had, for the first time in American history, been nominated for the Presidency by a major political party. Nor is it a coincidence that at about the same time the moral code for the new motion picture industry was drafted by a Roman Catholic priest; nor that shortly thereafter began a successful campaign to liberalize the nation's numerous anti-gambling and anti-lottery laws; nor that the same period saw a widespread relaxation of compulsory Sunday observance laws, particularly in respect to sports and entertainment in the afternoon (i.e., after church services).

It must be emphasized that there is no intent here to pass judgment as between Protestant and Catholic moral standards. As will shortly be seen, in respect to sexual morality Roman Catholicism has become more puritanic than has Protestantism. What is suggested here is only that there is a substantial difference between these two moral codes (and between them and that of American Judaism) and that the moral code of Roman Catholicism appears at the present time to be on the ascendant while that of Protestantism appears to be on the defensive.

It was the moral standards and values of New England Puritanism that Protestant dissent inherited and carried to the ever-expanding frontier and thus throughout the growing nation. The moral standards of Virginian Anglicanism were vastly different. As Justice Frankfurter noted in the *Miracle* case, when Anglicanism controlled England's churches James I's *Book of Sports* was required reading in the churches, while under the Puritans all copies were consigned to the flames. But Anglicanism had little influence in shaping either America's morality or culture. It was the Puritan scale of moral values that prevailed and in this scale the important virtues were honesty, industry, thrift, austerity, and Godliness, while the major

evils were frivolity, gambling, extravagance, dishonesty, sexual immorality, and Sabbath-breaking.

Not all these evils could be translated into terms of secular law;
it is not feasible, for example, to make frivolity or thriftlessness a
penal offense. To the extent, however, that the compulsory arm of
the law could be employed to impose Puritan moral values upon
the community at large, it was done. The countless state laws against
traffic in obscene books, gambling and lotteries, adultery and other
sex crimes, licentiousness and Sabbath-breaking, all witness to the
monopolistic domination that Puritan Protestantism has exercised
over America's penal codes. The prominent role that Protestant clergymen like Charles H. Parkhurst and John Haynes Holmes have
played in the struggle against corruption in municipal government
is another indication of the high estate held by honesty in the Protestant scale of moral values.

These are the traditional moral values of Calvinist New England
taken over and somewhat expanded by Protestant dissent (to include
strong opposition to liquor consumption) so as to become the
moral values of pan-Protestantism. As we shall see, the influences
of secular humanism have lately effected a noticeable modification
and change of emphasis in these values on the part of Protestantism.
The traditional moral values of Roman Catholicism have also been
affected by the influences of American secular humanism, but para-
doxically in a directly contrary way. Whereas they have made pan-
Protestantism less puritanic and more liberal, Roman Catholicism has
in some respects become less liberal and more puritanic in its reaction
to them. It is a sin for a Roman Catholic in New York to view the
allegedly immoral film *Baby Doll;* it is no sin if he views the same
picture in London or Paris. The motion picture *The Miracle* was
exhibited in Rome without objection by the Church which, under
the terms of the Lateran agreements with the Vatican, could have
prevented its exhibition by raising objections; the same film was
banned to Catholics by Cardinal Spellman in America. Perhaps only
in Ireland is puritanism so potent a force in Catholic moral values
as it is in the United States.

Nevertheless, the overall standard of moral values even in American Catholicism is more liberal than that of pan-Protestantism; the
puritanism of American Roman Catholicism is on the whole limited
to the area of sexual relations. Consumption of intoxicating liquors
and engaging in gambling do not of themselves violate Catholic

morality. The smoking of cigarettes is not looked on with disfavor as it is in some Protestant denominations. Roman Catholicism, even in America, does not frown upon frivolity nor exalt austerity. Sports and amusements are permissible even on the Sabbath. Standards of honesty and truthfulness are more flexible than those avowed by Protestantism.

Of all the major faiths in America, the moral standards of Judaism are closest to those of secular humanism. Since the disappearance of the Essenes, perhaps into Christianity, asceticism has been alien to Jewish traditions. As a this-world religion, Judaism looks favorably on joyful living, particularly in its sabbaths and most of its holy days. It does not frown upon the consumption of liquor; the drinking of wine is a prescribed rite of every sabbath, holiday, and major religious event, such as circumcision and marriage. Austerity is not deemed particularly virtuous in American Judaism; nor is self-denial for its own sake considered desirable. Because both original sin and the innate wickedness of man are alien to Jewish concepts, there is no need or place in Judaism for a way of living that calls for a stringent curbing of the normal desires of man. Celibacy, exalted in Roman Catholicism, is frowned upon in Judaism. All in all, the concept of mortification of the flesh has no place in the moral code of American Judaism.

AN EXPERIMENT NOBLE IN MOTIVE

The Eighteenth Amendment represents the one major instance in which a religious body has used the force of law in an attempt to impose its own code of morality upon the entire nation. Earlier, Protestantism succeeded in obtaining passage of a Federal law banning the interstate transportation or mailing of lottery tickets; but this law, of course, did not forbid engaging in lotteries within the states. Earlier still, Protestantism played a prominent role in the abolitionist movement and the ultimate adoption of the Thirteenth Amendment banning slavery. Yet, slavery had been defended by a substantial part of the Protestant church, and it is almost certain that the combination of America's secular social conscience (as typified, for example, by Jefferson) and the nation's economic development would have brought an end to slavery even if Protestantism had never concerned itself with the issue.

The same is not true with respect to Prohibition. Charles and Mary Beard, in their *Rise of American Civilization*, suggest that the economic forces that contributed to the adoption of the Prohibition amendment are generally ignored or underestimated. They point out, for example, that the Prohibition movement was supported by businessmen in the South who sought increased sobriety and regularity on the part of their Negro workers, while elsewhere employers added their support because drunken workmen were a danger as well as an economic loss to machine industry. Charles Beard has been much criticized for overemphasizing economic motivations in history. Whether or not the criticism is otherwise merited, it is fair to suggest that in the present instance, the economic factor was of secondary and relatively minor significance. Had there been no united and highly efficient Protestantism behind the Prohibitionist movement, there would have been no Eighteenth Amendment, irrespective of the economic losses due to drunkardness. On the other hand, it is more than probable that the amendment would have been enacted even had the employer class remained indifferent. The Prohibition amendment came about because behind it was a determined, united, and effective Protestantism.

That Protestantism was determined is evidenced by the patience and persistence with which it pressed for outlawing traffic in liquor. Protestants established the National Temperance Society in 1865, and four years later entered into the political arena with the founding of the National Prohibition Party, committed to "the total prohibition of the manufacturing, importation and traffic of intoxicating beverages." In 1874 the Women's Christian Temperance Union was formed, to be followed in 1893 by the formation of the Anti-Saloon League, which called itself "the church in action against the saloon," and in 1916 by the Methodist Board of Temperance, Prohibition and Morals.

Protestantism was as united as it was determined. With the exception of the Protestant Episcopal Church, no major denomination in American Protestantism dissented either from opposition to consumption of and traffic in intoxicating liquors or from participation in political activity to translate that opposition into the law of the land. The Methodist Episcopal Church, South, for example, motivated no doubt in large measure by the prominent role played by Northern churches in the abolitionist movement, had long urged that the Church refrain from political activity. But when the issue of Prohibition came to the fore, the Church reversed itself completely and threw itself wholeheartedly into the fray.

And Protestantism was as effective as it was united and determined. At the height of its power it was probably the strongest and most effective political lobby in American history. The Anti-Saloon League alone had an annual budget that reached two and a half million dollars, contributed by some 30,000 Protestant churches and 60,000 co-operating agencies. Luke Ebersole, in his *Church Lobbying in the Nation's Capital*, quotes a writer in the Prohibition era who noted that "the average member of Congress is more afraid of the Anti-Saloon League than he is even of the President of the United States." By 1907 the fruits of the labors of united Protestantism began to ripen with the enactment of the first state prohibitory laws. By 1919 such laws were on the books of thirty-three states and during the same year the Eighteenth Amendment became part of the Constitution of the United States.

Protestants frequently express alarm at the vast political power and influence of the Roman Catholic Church. Yet, American Catholicism has never been powerful enough to obtain enactment or adoption of a controversial measure at the national level. The Catholic Church today still does not have the political power possessed by American Protestantism during the first quarter of the twentieth century.

The failure of what Herbert Hoover once called an "experiment noble in motive" has not altered the conviction of much of the Protestant church that prohibitory legislation is a morally correct (though perhaps not completely effective) way to deal with the problem of intoxicating liquors. Even today Protestant organizations agitate for state legislation restricting or barring traffic in liquor, or for national laws or regulations by the Federal Civil Aeronautics Authority forbidding the serving of liquor on airplanes.

In the light of this agitation it is interesting to attempt to reconcile Protestant approval of prohibitory legislation affecting intoxicating liquors (and gambling, as well) and Protestant opposition to the passage of laws against disseminating information on contraceptive birth control. In respect to the latter, Protestants contend that it is unfair for the Catholic Church to invoke the coercive arm of the secular state to bar from non-Catholics information deemed sinful only by Catholics. On the other hand, Protestants have no hesitation in invoking the coercive arm of the secular state to bar non-Protestants from consuming intoxicating liquors (or engaging in gambling).

This charge of inconsistency could perhaps be met by Protestantism with the rejoinder that while practice of contraceptive birth control by married couples concerns none but themselves, intoxication (and gambling) may seriously harm the wives and children of those engaging in it, and therefore constitutes not merely a religious but also a social evil. The difficulty with such an explanation is that it cannot easily be reconciled with Protestant support of compulsory Sunday closing laws and refusal to accept as a substitute laws requiring every person to rest at least one day in every seven but not requiring him to choose the Lord's Day for his day of rest.

The real explanation, I suggest, lies not in the fact that intoxication is a social evil while contraceptive birth control among married couples is not. It is rather in the fact that American Protestantism conceives the ideal society as one in which everybody is sober and diligent, shuns gambling, and scrupulously observes the Sabbath, whereas American Catholicism conceives it as one from which moderate consumption of liquors and moderate engaging in games of chance are not excluded, but wherein everyone shuns birth control and has large families. Each would willingly employ the instrumentality of law and government to achieve its conception of the ideal society. That, of course, is what is meant by competition among religious cultures.

BINGO

The Protestant war on legal gambling has been considerably less dramatic, and also less successful, than the war on legal drinking. Yet the sensational success of Protestantism in the Prohibition campaign was relatively short lived, while most of the fruits of its anti-gambling endeavors are still with us. How long they will remain is open to question. Although American Catholicism was more than unsympathetic to the Prohibition experiment, it made no determined effort to end it. Catholicism does, however, have an important stake in at least one form of gambling and in many communities has launched determined campaigns to liberalize the anti-gambling laws. Moreover, where it has undertaken these campaigns it has been almost uniformly successful. It is therefore reasonable to predict that here too Protestantism will suffer a substantial defeat at the hands of its competitor, even if it does not suffer the debacle experienced in the Prohibition experiment.

Interestingly enough, when Protestantism first launched its national campaign against gambling, it not only encountered no Catholic opposition but, on the contrary, had the active support of a substantial part of the Catholic Church. In 1894 a memorial against the lottery evil and in favor of a Federal anti-lottery law was presented to Congress by a host of Christian leaders, including Cardinal James Gibbons and three Roman Catholic archbishops. As late as 1941, Cardinal O'Connell of Boston joined forces with the Protestant church and with a number of Jewish clergymen in successfully opposing a proposal introduced in the Massachusetts legislature to conduct a state lottery as a means of raising revenue.

All this is history, hardly likely to repeat itself. Catholic co-operation marked the successful campaign for the enactment in 1894 of the Federal law prohibiting the interstate mailing or transportation of lottery tickets. It marked the successful campaign to defeat enactment of a state lottery law in Massachusetts in 1941. Undoubtedly Catholic clergymen had earlier co-operated in the campaigns that led to the enactment of anti-gambling and anti-lottery laws in almost all the states. But the overriding necessity on the part of the Catholic Church to maintain without the aid of tax-raised funds its gigantic and ever-expanding church and school system required a modification of the position taken by Cardinal Gibbons and Cardinal O'Connell.

The stand of these and other Catholic churchmen, it should be noted, represented simply Catholic accommodation to the mores and values of a Protestant culture; it was not required by anything in Catholic dogma or morality. According to *The Catholic Encyclopedia* a lottery is morally objectionable only "if carried to excess, as it tends to develop the gambling spirit and distract people from earning a livelihood by honest work. However, if there is no fraud of any sort in the transaction, and if there is some sort of proportion between the price of a ticket and the value of a chance of gaining a prize, a lottery cannot be condemned as in itself immoral." According to the column "Theology for Everyman," appearing in the *Pilot*, official organ of the Boston archdiocese, "No one can be accused of sin merely because he plays cards for money, or because he buys lottery tickets, or because he lays wagers on races or other athletic contests. It is quite possible that actions such as these may take place in completely unobjectionable circumstances and may serve the purposes of harmless, or even helpful recreation."

Bingo had apparently been invented during the thirties by movie theater owners to be used along with double features, amateur nights, and free dishware as a means to entice an apparently unwilling public into their theaters. Its rise in popularity was almost phenomenal, and many hard-pressed priests began to look enviously at the long lines of persons willing to pay to enter a movie house primarily to play bingo. It was quite natural that some of them would reason that if the public was willing to pay in order to play bingo in movie houses there was no reason to believe it would not pay to play the same game of chance in parish houses.

In any event, without premeditation and without design, Catholic parishes all over the country spontaneously took up bingo. Innumerable churches set up their "bingo nights" once (usually Sunday) and frequently twice or more each week. Catholic mothers, who previously had gone to the movies after feeding their children and putting them to bed, now went to the church to play bingo. The annual *Official Catholic Directory* began to print full-page colored advertisements by manufacturers of the equipment used in bingo. In Cincinnati in one year alone (1939) some thirty Catholic churches netted a profit of almost $1,500,000 out of bingo played by some two and a half million players.

It must not be supposed that this development was welcomed by all Catholic churchmen. Many have had grave reservations and many have actively opposed it. But on the whole the Church has accepted it, perhaps as a necessity. The selling of "raffles" and "chances" has long been an accepted method of raising funds to maintain the parish, and bingo was hardly any different. In any event, the overwhelming majority of Catholic church leaders now endorse bingo and support campaigns to make it legal. In many communities representatives of the Church have sought—sometimes successfully, sometimes not—to prevail upon police officials not to enforce the anti-gambling laws against churches engaged in bingo. In New York City in 1954 a high police official was demoted and shortly thereafter resigned after arousing a storm of protest for his strict enforcement of the anti-gambling law against bingo playing in Catholic churches.

Catholic church leaders have pushed for the enactment of laws allowing bingo and similar games of chance where all the proceeds inure to the benefit of religious and charitable organizations. Protestant church groups have been unanimously opposed to such permissive legislation. In this struggle Catholicism has been uniformly successful and Protestantism has uniformly failed. State after state and community after community are adopting permissive bingo laws. But perhaps the best measure of Catholic success lies in the fact that among the issues deemed by Governor Averell Harriman sufficiently important to be called to the attention of the New York State legislature in his 1957 annual message the following was included:

Two years ago I recommended that statutory provisions be made for churches and other bona fide charitable organizations to conduct games of bingo, provided that the entire proceeds were devoted to charitable purposes. There was precedent for such statutory action, but the [Republican controlled] Legislature chose to follow the slower process of constitutional amendment to attain the same end.

I call your attention to the fact that the amendment passed in 1955 must be passed again this year, if action is again not to be deferred for two years. In addition, I urge that the legislation needed to implement the constitutional change should be enacted at this session so that there may be no delay if the people approve the amendment at the polls this fall.

A word should be added concerning the Jewish position on this issue. In general, rabbinic and synagogue organizations have kept aloof from the struggle. However, in 1955 both the New York Board of Rabbis and the United Synagogue, the latter representing the synagogues affiliated with the Conservative branch of Judaism, by formal resolution disapproved of the use of bingo and other games of chance as a means to raise funds for synagogue and religious school purposes. In 1958 the Reform congregational organization followed suit. None of these groups, however, expressed any opinion as to the desirability of legislation either prohibiting or permitting bingo for the benefit of religious and charitable agencies. It is probable that the views expressed by these three organizations represent the position of American Jewry, both in respect to what was said and what was left unsaid.

OBSCENITY AND CENSORSHIP

America's sexual code—or its professed code—is inherited from Deuteronomy via New England Calvinism. In England the puritanism of the Cromwellian interregnum was largely mitigated by the extreme liberality of the Restoration, but the Restoration had no significant influence in the American colonies. It was not until America breathed of the spirit of the French Enlightenment in the last quarter of the eighteenth century that it witnessed some relaxation in the severity of Calvinist puritanism in the area of sexual morality. But while Protestant dissent could make common cause with the French Enlightenment in achieving religious and political liberty and an egalitarian society, they were poles apart in their standards of an acceptable code of sexual morality. The respite from the severity of New England puritanism in the post-Revolutionary War period was brief and left no noticeable influence. The organization in 1802 of the Society for the Suppression of Vice, in 1813 of the Society for the Reformation of Morals, and in 1825 of the American Tract Society—all under Protestant sponsorship—marked the triumphant return of New England puritanism to the field of America's sexual moral standards.

As we have seen, Protestant concepts of the relationship of church and state did not exclude the use of organized Protestant church pressure to translate into secular law Protestant abhorrence of intoxicating liquors and gambling. But these excursions into the political arena were simply latter-day renewals of a campaign long earlier commenced. In 1821, decades before the first anti-liquor or anti-gambling law appeared on the books of any American state, New England Protestantism prevailed upon the Vermont legislature to enact the first state law in the United States making it a criminal offense to publish or exhibit obscene matter. Shortly thereafter two other New England states—Massachusetts and Connecticut—followed suit. From New England the anti-obscenity crusade spread throughout the nation so that today every state of the union has some kind of anti-obscenity statute on its books. On the national level a provision was added to the Tariff Act of 1842 prohibiting the import of obscene books, and in 1872, as result of the pressure of a militant Protestantism led by Anthony Comstock, the first of a series of laws was passed barring obscene matter from the mails and from interstate transportation. It was, however, not until 1957 that the constitutionality of anti-obscenity laws was settled by two definitive decisions of the United States Supreme Court.

Protestantism was not content with securing the enactment of these laws; it made every effort to see that they were enforced. Organizations such as the New York Society for the Suppression of Vice and the New England Watch and Ward Society constituted themselves self-appointed quasi-public officials to act as guardians of the people's morals. How they operated is described in the following words by a Federal court in granting an injunction against the Watch and Ward Society:

The defendant [Rev. J. Franklin] Chase and the society of which he is secretary scrutinize publications of various kinds, including books and magazines. If they believe that a book or article violates the [anti-obscenity] law, they inform the large distributors of their opinion, with the intimation, express or implied, that if the book or magazine be sold or distributed prosecution will follow. Where this warning is ignored, it is their custom to institute prosecution. . . .

This procedure, employed also by another arm of Protestantism, the Lord's Day Alliance, in enforcing Sunday laws, long antedated the Catholics' creation of the National Office for Decent Literature (formed in 1938 by the Catholic bishops in the United States under the title National Organization for Decent Literature and often called N.O.D.L.).

To get an idea of the effect and effectiveness of the Protestant anti-obscenity crusade one need only look at a sampling of the books that were at one time or another banned from the mails or suppressed under state laws. The list of books subject to Protestant-inspired censorship includes such works as Tolstoy's *Kreutzer Sonata*, Rousseau's *Confessions*, Swedenborg's *Amor Conjugalis*, Joyce's *Ulysses*, Dreiser's *The Genius* and *American Tragedy*, Cabell's *Jurgen*, Sinclair Lewis' *Elmer Gantry*, Hemingway's *The Sun Also Rises*, and H. G. Wells's *The World of William Clissold*. Again it must be emphasized that all this took place long before the Catholic Church in America interested itself in secular censorship.

One thing should become apparent during the course of this book: competition among religious cultures has its effects upon the competitors. Protestantism, Catholicism, and Judaism borrow from one another and all three borrow from secular humanism. Even if their basic dogma and basic way-of-life concepts are not radically changed, they are continually being modified, at least on the surfaces. We have seen, for example, how American Catholicism adapted itself to accept a modified concept of church-state separation and how it has changed its position on so vital an issue as the teaching of religion in the public schools. We have seen how Judaism eagerly accepted the American system of church-state separation, a relationship completely alien to its 3,000-year history. We have seen how Protestantism accepted, even though reluctantly, the transformation of its own religious school system into a basically secular school system.

Something similar is happening to Protestantism in the field of anti-obscenity censorship. Protestantism has not receded from its puritan doctrine of the sinfulness of obscenity. While this particular evil does not play as prominent a part in Protestant public pronouncements as it formerly did, Protestant clergymen evince little hesitation in joining interfaith committees to urge vendors to refrain from selling and readers to refrain from purchasing obscene literature (although they are undoubtedly considerably more liberal than their fathers and grandfathers in judging a book obscene). What much of American Protestantism does seem to have given up is the idea of compulsion. There are, of course, many individual Protestant clergymen who see nothing improper and much that is desirable in Federal and state laws for the censorship or suppression of obscene publications. But a great part of American Protestantism has veered away from coercive censorship. In 1953 the Baptist Stanley Stuber, in his *Primer on Roman Catholicism for Protestants*, could say with some realism that "Protestants believe the conscience of the individual Christian should be the guide in the reading of books and the viewing of plays, movies and television. . . ." In the days of the strong-arm tactics of Anthony Comstock and the Rev. J. Franklin Chase such a statement would have been almost laughable.

As Protestantism's obscenity-obsession receded, Catholicism's became increasingly acute. The Catholic Church took up where the Protestant church left off. Nothing in Catholic dogma—as nothing in Calvinist dogma—militated against employing the coercive arm of secular government to impose upon all citizens the Church's concepts of Christian morality, and the Catholic N.O.D.L. has today as little hesitation in co-operating with the police or instigating police action against what it deems obscene publications as had the Protestant Watch and Ward Society or the Protestant Society for the Suppression of Vice.

Perhaps because Catholicism had the benefit of Protestantism's experience in the war against immoral literature, or perhaps because of its own superior organizational structure, it is proving more effective than was Protestantism in the enforcement of Protestantism's moral standards and its anti-obscenity laws. It operates nationally as well as locally; its National Legion of Decency (though administered by the New York Archdiocese) and N.O.D.L. are national and not, like the Society for the Suppression of Vice or the Watch and Ward Society, merely local agencies.

Nor has Catholicism been content to limit itself to police action; it operates on many levels. Beginning with the original Motion Picture Production Code, it was Catholic influence that for more than two decades dominated, and continues to dominate, the moral standards of American motion picture production.

In addition, Catholicism borrowed from labor unionism the technique of the boycott, just as it borrowed from Protestantism the technique of semi-official police action; and here too it bettered the instruction it had received. The law does not permit labor unions to engage in what are called secondary boycotts. A union may boycott a manufacturer who produces a non-union product, and it may boycott the product; but it may not boycott all the products of another manufacturer simply because he uses one non-union product, nor boycott all the products of a storekeeper merely because one of these products was made by a non-union employer. The Catholic Church operates under no such limitations. The late Cardinal Dougherty of Philadelphia warned two theater owners that if they persisted in exhibiting two allegedly immoral pictures (*The Outlaw* and *Forever Amber*) their theaters would be boycotted for an entire year. The Diocesan office at Duluth declared a boycott against a theater for six months.

Catholicism, moreover, is making a concerted effort at something that Protestantism never very much bothered with: the involvement of the other faiths. Catholicism's general antipathy to interfaith committees appears to be subordinated to what it deems the more important end of suppressing immorality. Catholic priests and Catholic laymen under priestly guidance take the lead in forming citizens' committees for decent literature and similar interfaith groups. (Msgr. Thomas J. Fitzgerald, executive secretary of N.O.D.L., makes it a special point to inform the public that its reviewing board includes both a Protestant and a Jewish reviewer.) An effort is made to involve Protestant and Jewish clergymen who, notwithstanding frequent inner reservations and discomfort, often find it impossible to refuse to co-operate.

It must not be supposed that there has been no dissent within Catholicism from this new crusade. Walter Kerr, in one of a series of articles in *Commonweal* (the entire series was later published in book form under the title *Catholicism in America*), inveighed against what he called the "purity-with-popcorn" level of Catholic taste in motion pictures. The Rev. John Courtney Murray expressed concern about some of the strong-arm tactics of "voluntary agencies which exercise some measure of surveillance, judgment, and even control of various media of communication," and that in the excesses of their campaign against obscenity Catholics may find themselves in the camp of the philistines.

But there can be little doubt about the position of American Catholicism on the issue. *Commonweal,* published by laymen, has little significant influence on church thinking. Father Murray's strictures were mild and he promptly came to the defense of the N.O.D.L. when John Fischer, editor of *Harper's Magazine,* sought to read out of these strictures a lesson for that organization. The Legion of Decency and the N.O.D.L. are ecclesiastical organizations having the full support of the entire Church. The anti-smut activities of Catholic lay organizations, such as the Catholic War Veterans or the National Council of Catholic Men, invariably have either priestly instigation or priestly approval. It is fairly clear that the crusade against obscenity has become the prized, and is on the way of becoming exclusively, the possession of American Catholicism.

In some respects this turn of events is surprising. It is true that among the eleven categories of books prohibited to Catholics by the Canon Law are included (as the ninth) books "which have for their principal purpose the description, narration, or teaching of matter lascivious or obscene." But this is an extremely liberal prohibition (note the qualifying adjective "principal"), far more liberal than the practical standards of the Legion of Decency and the N.O.D.L. Moreover, the Catholic anti-obscenity crusade is a comparatively recent venture. Finally, as Father Murray pointed out, Catholics "stand, not only within the oldest religious tradition of the Western world, but also within its most venerable tradition of intellect, literature, and art," a tradition that has produced great achievements not all of which are "fit for children."

American Catholic prudery in literature and art is in marked contrast to the general approach of European Continental Catholicism. (*Letters from My Windmill* and *The Miracle*, films condemned by the American Legion of Decency, were praised by equivalent Catholic agencies in France and Italy.) It does, however, correspond to the prudery and puritanism of the Catholicism of Ireland, and the explanation for the American venture may lie, in whole or in part, in the domination of American Catholicism by clergy of Irish ethnic background. The difficulty with this explanation lies in the fact that the anti-obscenity crusade is becoming increasingly intense just when Catholics of Italian background are rapidly emerging as serious rivals, threatening the more than century-old hegemony of the Irish.

I suggest the real explanation lies in terms of the consequences of cultural competition. Except where precluded by unalterable or relatively unalterable dogma or church structure (e.g., exclusive ecclesiastical control of church worship, office and property) or of overriding financial considerations (e.g., bingo), American Catholicism (like American Judaism) tends to adopt American cultural patterns, and in the area of avowed moral standards these patterns have been shaped by the puritanism of New England Calvinism. This point will come up again in later chapters and will be discussed more fully in the concluding chapter of this book. Here it is sufficient to list, for the purpose of comparison with the previously mentioned literary works subjected to Protestant-inspired censorship, the following sampling of works on the N.O.D.L. listing of banned books: Erskine Caldwell's *God's Little Acre*, James T. Farrell's *A World I Never Made*, Hemingway's *To Have and Have Not*, Huxley's *Antic Hay*, Christopher Isherwood's *The World in the Evening*, D. H. Lawrence's *Women in Love*, Richard Wright's *Native Son*, and Zola's *Nana*.

In accommodating itself to American cultural patterns Judaism has not adopted the puritanism of New England Calvinism. The reason, I think, lies partly in the long Jewish tradition of frank discussion of sex going back to the Bible and the Talmud. (In my teens I was a student at an Orthodox Jewish theological seminary and can testify that the frankness of the discussion of sexual matters in the course of my instruction would have astounded the most progressive of modern secular educators.) Partly the explanation lies in the close affinity of the American Jewish community to American secular humanism. Whatever the reason, there can be little doubt that, while occasionally a rabbi will be unable to refuse an invitation by his Christian colleagues to join in a local campaign against obscene publications, American Judaism has no sympathy for Catholicism's crusade.

Perhaps the best way to conclude this section is to relate two incidents that occurred in 1957. The first occurred in Syracuse, New York, where thirty Protestant ministers publicly criticized the two local newspapers for refusing to accept advertisements of the film *Baby Doll*, which had been attacked as immoral by Cardinal Spellman. The second occurred in the Massachusetts legislature. An antiobscenity bill was introduced and, after considerable discussion and pressure for and against, was passed in one house but defeated in the other. The details of the bill are not particularly relevant here. What is relevant and significant is the alignment for and against the measure. The bill was vigorously supported by the Roman Catholic archdiocese of Boston. It was opposed by the Massachusetts Council of Churches (Protestantism), the Boston Jewish Community Council and the American Jewish Congress (Judaism), and the Massachusetts Civil Liberties Union (secular humanism). The American experiment in cultural competition is indeed creative and dynamic.

BLUE SUNDAY

Logic would require consideration of Sunday laws in the chapter discussing religion and the state. It is dealt with here for two reasons. First, strict Sabbath observance was long considered by Protestantism as part of its moral code in the same category as abstinence from liquor, gambling, or sexual immorality. In the second place, the positions of the two major Christian churches on Sabbath laws and observance appear to be passing through the same changes as their positions on obscenity and censorship.

For three centuries Protestantism was the sole guardian of the Christian Sabbath. The various Sunday laws on the statute books of the states date from colonial times when Protestantism (Calvinism in New England, Anglicanism in Virginia) was joined to or was part of the state. Like the Anti-Saloon League, the Society for the Suppression of Vice and the Watch and Ward Society, Protestantism established an agency, the Lord's Day Alliance, to police enforcement of Sunday laws and resist efforts to liberalize the laws. For many years Protestantism's concern about Sabbath-breaking rivaled its concern about liquor drinking and immoral publications. And during the entire period Protestantism was as ready to use the secular arm of the state to enforce its concepts, against non-Protestants and indeed non-Christians, in the field of Sabbath breaking as in the field of traffic in intoxicating liquors, salacious publications, or lottery tickets.

In recent years, however, Protestantism appears to have yielded to Catholicism primary responsibility for guarding the Christian Sabbath just as it has yielded to Catholicism primary responsibility for guarding Christian morality. It may be that most Protestant clergymen are still committed to the moral correctness of state-enforced anti-liquor, anti-gambling, and anti-obscenity laws. But in large measure, interest in Sunday laws and their enforcement has dropped to secondary importance in the Protestant hierarchy of interests; the Lord's Day Alliance has become a stepchild of American Protestantism. The Catholic Church has become the new champion.

Nothing in Catholic dogma requires the Church to undertake a Sabbath-observance crusade of the type in which it is now engaged. Catholic ecclesiastical law requires only that the faithful attend Mass on Sunday and abstain from unnecessary servile work. Neither participation in sports nor performance of secular work—both anathema to New England Puritanism—are barred by Canon Law. Catholicism's venture in the field of Protestant-type Sabbath observance is of even more recent origin than its venture in the field of anti-obscenity activities. Here, too, as in the anti-obscenity crusade, the explanation lies in terms of adjustment to American patterns as a consequence of cultural competition. In April, 1957, Catholic Bishop John J. Wright of Worcester, Massachusetts, publicly lauded "the Protestant tradition" for the fact that New England did not have the Sunday shopping problem besetting other parts of the country. "A Protestant Christian ethic is reflected," he said, "since the legislation dates from the days when a Protestant theocracy governed the writing of the basic laws of the region."

Catholicism has not up to the present time set up a policing agency in the field of Sabbath observance analogous to the Legion of Decency or the N.O.D.L. It does, however, employ the other techniques it has perfected, including the interfaith committee. Catholic sponsors of these interfaith committees evince no sense of incongruity or unfairness in inviting Jewish merchants and rabbis to join in these interfaith committees for the compulsory observance of the Christian Sabbath.

Although these Jewish merchants and rabbis occasionally feel they cannot refuse such invitations, the position of the organized Jewish community, clerical, congregational and secular, is in opposition to compulsory Sunday laws. These are deemed an unwarranted infringement upon the religious liberty of non-Christians and inconsistent with the requirements of church-state separation. While a number of states do have provisions in their Sunday laws exempting from the operation of those laws persons who observe a day other than Sunday as their religious day of rest, most state Sunday laws do not. The absence of such an exemption is particularly resented by organized Judaism.

This brief consideration of Sunday laws and observance can best be concluded, as was the previous section, with the recounting of an incident that occurred recently, this time in New York. It illustrates the same point. For some time there has been pending in the legislatures of both the state and the city of New York bills to amend the Sunday law so as to exempt Jewish and Seventh Day Adventist merchants who keep their stores closed on Saturdays. The measures have the support of the State Council of Churches (Protestant) and the Protestant Council of New York (both of which oppose all other relaxations of the law), all the Jewish organizations, and the New York Civil Liberties Committee. It failed of passage in 1958 because of the determined opposition of the Catholic Church.

7. THE FAMILY AND THE CHILD

CHURCH DOGMA AND FAMILY WELFARE

In no area of public policy does religious dogma assert itself more vigorously than in the domain of family and child welfare. On certain other issues, as has been pointed out in the preceding pages, American Catholicism and the Protestant-humanist alliance have achieved at least a tacit compromise. There is, however, no prospect of a comparable meeting of minds on such controversial questions as birth control, therapeutic abortion, artificial insemination, divorce, or adoption across religious lines.

This is understandable for a number of reasons. Protestants, Jews, and humanists consider the individual to be the basic social unit. To the Catholic Church, both conceptually and practically, it is the family. The family is deemed a holy institution. In the words of Pius XI, it "is more sacred than the state." Much is made in Catholic teachings of the "Holy Family" of Jesus, although as far as the text of the Gospels reveals, the relationship of Jesus to his mother and brothers (cousins, according to Catholic dogma) was far from ideal. Matrimony is a sacrament and the relationship of husband and wife is analogized to that of Christ and his Church, the husband representing Christ and the wife the Church. The high place held by authority in the Catholic hierarchy of values is reflected in the emphasis placed by the Church on parental rights.

Practical considerations point in the same direction, particularly in the United States. Here constitutional requirements of separation of church and state bar direct grants of tax-raised funds to the Church or to church schools. By elevating the family to the status

112.

of the basic social unit, a way may be found to overcome the constitutional barriers. Education, for example, is declared by the Church in the United States to be a function not of the state but of the family. (In countries where there is no problem of church-state separation it is declared to be a function of the Church.) Hence, it is entirely proper for the family to decide what type of school its children shall attend. If it chooses a private rather than a state school, the state quite properly should pay the family the money thus saved.

The practical consequences of Catholic elevation of the family are many. Several will become apparent throughout the chapter. Here two will be mentioned simply for illustrative purposes. The first is Catholic opposition not only to divorce (which, of course, is unyielding and uncompromising) but also to separation. Non-Catholic social workers dealing with family and marital problems also strive to prevent the breakup of the family unit. But the difference is that to the Protestant, Jewish, and secular social agency, maintenance of the unbroken family unit is a means to an end, the happiness of the individual members of the family. To Catholicism, however, it is an end in itself, to be served even at the cost of the happiness of the individual members. The second illustrative consequence was the strong opposition of the Catholic Church to the proposed Anti-Child Labor Amendment, which the Church considered an unwarranted intrusion upon the sanctity and sovereignty of the family.

This leads to another reason for the depth of the division between Protestantism and Catholicism in America on the issues discussed in this chapter. The liberal position that American Protestantism takes on them is not compelled by anything inherent in Protestantism, certainly not Calvinist Protestantism. (It was the Protestant-inspired Comstock law that made unlawful the transportation across state lines or through the mail of contraceptive devices or information.) This liberalism was born out of secular humanism, which substantially transformed Protestantism (like Judaism) from an other-world to a this-world religion, a religion in which temporal happiness and welfare is a good to be sought for all, or for as many as possible. Family planning, therapeutic abortion, artificial insemination, divorce where continued cohabitation would lead to further unhappiness, adoption of orphans or illegitimate children by couples likely to assure them a happy home and happy life—all these are desirable ends now deemed consistent with religious obligations.

Catholicism's accommodation to American culture values, on the other hand, has been limited mainly to the Calvinist elements, such as sexual morality, Sabbath observance and, but for overriding economic considerations, opposition to gambling. Catholicism has made little adjustment to the secular-humanist elements (although its rather reluctant acceptance of non-contraceptive or "rhythm" birth control may constitute such an adjustment). It remains primarily a next-world religion. To Catholicism welfare means mainly eternal, rather than temporal, welfare; and happiness means mainly happiness after death, rather than before. Since contraceptive birth control, therapeutic abortion, artificial insemination, divorce, or adoption of a Catholic-born child by a non-Catholic couple would or might result in loss of eternal salvation, they are to be strongly condemned and opposed irrespective of considerations of temporal welfare and this-world happiness.

A third reason for the apparently unbridgeable gap between Catholicism and non-Catholicism in the family welfare area are the Catholic concepts of morality and natural law—concepts that non-Catholics have great difficulty in understanding and greater difficulty in appreciating. This will be further considered in the following section on birth control. Here it need only be noted, first, that much of what the Catholic Church considers immoral is not so considered by Protestantism or Judaism, and certainly not by secular humanism, and second, that the concept of natural law is really a medium for the translation of the cultural concepts of a particular religious group into imperatives for the entire community.

BIRTH CONTROL

When the Comstock law of 1873 included among its prohibitions the interstate transportation of contraceptive materials or literature, no cry of protest was to be heard from Protestant sources. By 1932 the Federal Council of Churches had reached a point of view toward contraceptive birth control which can best be described as one of benevolent neutrality. The question, it said, "should be re-examined dispassionately, from the point of view of morality and hygiene, with due regard to the best means of maintaining desirable standards of living and fully discharging the fundamental obligations of parents to each other and to their children." Today there is hardly a planned parenthood committee in the nation that does not include at least one Protestant minister in its membership. With many Protestant clergymen the cycle has made a complete turn and what was morally prohibited in 1873 has become morally obligatory today. Said Bishop G. Bromley Oxnam:

When we make available to mothers sound scientific information which is used for the high moral objective of bringing to our families healthy, happy children, we are wisely using scientific means for moral ends. Religious leaders are awake to the dangers of family life which planned parenthood can help to correct. Communities which fail to provide proper marriage counseling, sex education, and child spacing service are recreant to their trust.

Even more emphatic was Dean James A. Pike of the Cathedral of St. John the Divine in New York (now Bishop of the Protestant Episcopal Diocese of California). When a married couple do not want a child, he told a planned parenthood meeting in 1955, they have a moral and religious obligation to practice contraceptive birth control rather than bear an unwanted child. "To do less," he said, "is to fail to worship God with 'our whole mind' as well as with our whole heart; to fail to exercise the stewardship of the lives which He has committed to our charge."

Whether so extreme a view is shared by the majority of Protestant clergymen cannot be said, although it is a fair guess that it finds much favor among the younger clergy. It is certain that at the very least Protestantism does not consider the issue either moral or theological and holds to the position that whether or not a married couple should engage in contraceptive birth control is a question which they have a right to decide for themselves without state or ecclesiastical interference. Hence, Protestantism is unanimous in its opposition to laws prohibiting responsible dissemination of birth control information and sale of materials.

This too is the position of American Judaism. To the liberal wing no theological question is involved in any case, and the basic moral problem is the prevention of the evils of uncontrolled parenthood. Reform rabbis, like Protestant ministers, are frequently found on planned parenthood committees. To the Orthodox wing, theological difficulties are present, since contraception when practiced by the male is forbidden by Talmudic authorities. However, even Orthodox

Judaism does not consider intervention by the state justified or justifiable.

To the Catholic Church contraceptive birth control is not merely sinful; it is a violation of natural law. According to Catholic doctrine, natural law is that part of moral law that guides human conduct and is the same at all times and places. It can be known to human reason without divine revelation. It is therefore binding not only upon Catholics nor even only upon Christians but upon all human beings. According to Pope Pius XI, "Any use whatsoever of marriage exercised in such a way that the act is deliberately frustrated in its natural power to generate life is an offense against the law of God and of nature." The purpose of marriage and the purpose of the sexual urge committed to man and woman by God is the propagation of the species. Satisfaction of the sexual urge in a way that artificially prevents conception aborts God's purpose and violates natural law.

For that reason the Catholic Church finds nothing wrong in its opposition to any laws that would permit dissemination of birth control information. Contraceptive birth control is immoral and the Church has as much right to oppose legislation permitting immoral practices as the Protestant church has in opposing legislation permitting immoral publications. Moreover, contraceptive birth control is not only immoral and unnatural in itself but also brings with it a host of other evils. It necessarily leads to moral and religious degeneration. It results in small families, fornication and adultery, hostile relationships between parent and child, and impairment of the welfare of the married couple. The fact that non-Catholics may not agree that these consequences ensue from contraceptive birth control does not and should not deter Catholics, who believe that they do, from acting politically on the basis of that belief.

Even more justified, according to the Catholic view, is the refusal of the Catholic Church to take part in community chest and fund-raising campaigns in which planned parenthood agencies also participate. If contraceptive birth control is immoral and unnatural according to Church dogma, how can the Church be expected to urge the faithful to contribute funds, part of which will be used to promote such immoral and unnatural purpose? Catholic withdrawal from these community chests may and often does have unfortunate consequences, in respect both to the effectiveness of the fund-raising campaign and to interfaith relationships between Catholics and non-

Catholics. The Church deeply deplores these consequences, but it could hardly act differently and yet be consistent with its conscience and its faith.

For the same reason the Church finds nothing wrong in barring the facilities of its hospitals to physicians who are members of planned parenthood associations (or who practice abortion or artificial insemination). This reasoning the non-Catholic observer finds more difficult to accept. Catholic hospitals are tax-exempt; as such they receive police, fire, and other costly services paid out of the taxes of all, non-Catholics as well as Catholics. If they accept these benefits they would appear to be under a reciprocal obligation to offer their services to all taxpayers, including those whose religious convictions do not preclude contraceptive birth control (or therapeutic abortion or artificial insemination). This obligation seems even clearer where the Catholic hospital receives direct governmental subsidies out of tax-raised funds, as under the Federal Hill-Burton Act.

Although Catholicism regards contraceptive birth control as violating the law of nature and therefore as evil and immoral even if practiced by non-Catholics, it has not so far made any determined effort to obtain enactment of laws prohibiting dissemination of birth control information or articles. It has contended itself with strenuously—and effectively—opposing efforts to repeal or modify the prohibitory laws in Massachusetts and Connecticut, the two states that have such laws on their books, and to oppose co-operation by the United States Government in bringing such information to the inhabitants of overpopulated foreign countries.

ABORTION

The division among the faiths with respect to contraceptive birth control is paralleled by their division on the issue of therapeutic abortion, i.e., abortion deemed necessary to save the mother's life or protect her from grave illness. The official position of Roman Catholicism was stated in 1930 by Pius XI in his encyclical letter, *Casti Connubi:*

However much we may pity the mother whose health and even life is

gravely imperiled in the performance of the duty allotted to her by na-
ture, nevertheless what could ever be sufficient reason for excusing in any
way the direct murder of the innocent? This is precisely what we are
dealing with here. Whether inflicted upon mother or upon the child, it
is against the precept of God and the law of nature: "Thou shalt not
kill." The life of each is equally sacred, and no one has the power, not
even the public authority, to destroy it.

Notwithstanding the assertion that "not even the public authority" may permit a therapeutic abortion and that it is against "the
law of nature" and hence an obligation binding on non-Catholics as
well as Catholics, the Church has also made no effort thus far to
obtain enactment of laws prohibiting therapeutic abortion. This is
possibly because the Church recognizes that its position is so unacceptable to the American people generally that an effort to translate it into law would not only be futile but would alienate many
non-Catholics. Or the reason may be—and this is probably the reason
the Church would give—that with the advance of medical science
the problem of therapeutic abortion is more theoretic than real.
Medicine has reached such an advanced stage of development that a
physician is rarely faced with the terrible dilemma of choosing between the life of the mother and the life of the child. Moreover,
as is also frequently urged in defense of the Catholic position, in
those rare cases where an abortion is indicated, the situation is almost
always such as would justify an indirect abortion, i.e., one where the
direct purpose of the operation is to remove a diseased condition in
the mother even though this removal indirectly causes the death of
the foetus, and such operation is permissible under Catholic Canon
Law.

While Catholicism does not seek to impose its views on therapeutic abortion on non-Catholics through the enactment of prohibitory laws, it does rigidly enforce these views in its own hospitals.
Catholic hospitals, like all other Catholic welfare institutions, are
ecclesiastically controlled and operated and are primarily religious
institutions. As Archbishop Edward F. Hoban of Cleveland said in
May, 1957, in an address at a convention of the Catholic Hospital
Association of the United States and Canada, "the ultimate and essential purpose of the Catholic hospital is the same as that of the Catholic Church—the sanctification and salvation of souls." If in a Catholic

hospital an unavoidable choice should have to be made between saving a patient's life and saving his soul, there can be only one acceptable answer: the soul must be saved even at the cost of the life, else the end would be sacrificed to save the means, for, as Pius XI said, "men are begotten not for the earth and for time, but for Heaven and eternity."

Insofar as Catholics, or at least adult Catholics, are concerned, non-Catholics have no more right to take issue with this decision than with the decision of adult Christian Scientists to reject all medical attention—a decision far more serious from the secular humanist viewpoint than the rare instance of choice between a Catholic's life and his soul. In a democracy committed to religious freedom such choices, except in the most extreme cases (illustrated by laws forbidding snake-handling cults), must be left to the individual. If the individual Catholic adult freely elects to enter a Catholic hospital with knowledge that if the dilemma should arise, the hospital would choose the soul over the life, that is a matter for the Catholic patient who, obviously, can enter a non-Catholic hospital if he wishes to.

As was suggested in the previous section, the issue is complicated by the fact that Catholic hospitals universally enjoy tax exemption and frequently also receive direct subsidies out of tax-raised funds. Acceptance of such benefits from the general public would seem to impose an obligation upon the hospital to serve the general public in accordance with the wishes of the general public, limited only by the secular laws enacted by the legislative representatives of the general public. The Catholic position is even more difficult to defend in communities where the municipally-owned (and frequently only) hospital is either operated under Catholic influence or is leased to the Catholic Church and operated by it as any Catholic-owned hospital (as, for example, in Jersey City, New Jersey).

It is certain that the Catholic position on therapeutic abortion is not shared by non-Catholics and does not reflect generally accepted American values. Every state in the Union has laws forbidding criminal abortion, but no court has interpreted these laws to encompass therapeutic abortion or is likely to do so. Nor is there neutrality on the question; Protestantism and Judaism (and, of course, secular humanism) are as committed to the principle that therapeutic abortion is morally mandatory as Catholicism is committed to the principle that it is morally prohibited.

EUTHANASIA, STERILIZATION, ARTIFICIAL
INSEMINATION

Of the three faiths only Catholicism has a definite and ascertainable position on euthanasia, sterilization, and artificial insemination (if it involves a donor other than the husband). In all cases Catholicism condemns the practice not merely for Catholics but, as immoral and violative of natural law, for non-Catholics as well. Euthanasia is condemned for the same reason that therapeutic abortion is condemned: it is the destruction of a human life, an act which is within God's exclusive jurisdiction except where the possessor has forfeited his right to retain it (capital punishment) or where necessary for the defense of the state (war). Eugenic as well as therapeutic sterilization is an interference with divine and natural law and is immoral even where performed pursuant to the decree of a court in a state which provides for compulsory sterilization of the congenitally criminal insane. Artificial insemination, according to Catholic dogma, is immoral both because it is adultery and because it normally involves masturbation, which is in itself an unnatural and immoral perversion of the sexual faculty.

Euthanasia is not permitted by law in any state (although it is common knowledge in the medical profession that it is often practiced privately). Proposals for the enactment of permissive euthanasia laws, conditioned upon the dying patient's request and certification by competent medical authority that his condition is incurable, are strongly opposed by the Catholic Church.

Therapeutic sterilization, i.e., sterilization performed to prevent pregnancy that may be dangerous to the mother's life or health, is not prohibited by any state law. The Church, as in the case of contraceptive birth control and therapeutic abortion, is making no effort to enact prohibitory laws, but limits itself to enforcing its policy in hospitals that it controls.

Compulsory or eugenic sterilization laws have been enacted in twenty-six states. Their constitutionality was upheld by a decision of the United States Supreme Court in 1927 on the ground, in the words of Justice Holmes, that "three generations of imbeciles are enough," and that it is within the police power of a state to prevent the perpetuation of hereditary criminality. Whether the 1927 decision would be upheld today is far from certain; considerable doubt on its continued validity was cast by a 1942 decision of the Supreme

Court. The extent to which the law is enforced is also questionable. In any case, the Catholic Church vigorously opposes its extension to states which do not have it. Indeed, it goes further; it prohibits judges who are of the Catholic faith from applying the law in those jurisdictions that do have it.

The legal status of artificial insemination (employed as a substitute for adoption where the husband alone is sterile) is still in the process of formation. The legal question is whether the act constitutes adultery and whether the resultant offspring is to be considered the legitimate child of the husband. Proposals to permit artificial insemination (with the husband's consent) and to legitimatize the resultant offspring are vigorously opposed by the Catholic Church.

There appears to be no consistent position on any of these issues within Protestantism or Judaism (or even secular humanism). Protestant and Jewish clergymen will often be found on committees sponsoring euthanasia legislation, but it is quite likely that at least as many Protestant and Jewish clergymen oppose such legislation. The same is probably true of legislation on eugenic sterilization and artificial insemination.

SEX EDUCATION IN THE PUBLIC SCHOOLS

The Catholic Church is vigorously opposed to sex education in the public schools. In 1949 the New York State Catholic Welfare Committee protested the exhibition in the public schools of two films, *Human Growth* and *Human Reproduction,* both endorsed by the state health commissioner and the state department of education. The Committee expressed its opposition to any attempt by the state "to usurp parental rights or to invade the sanctity of the home by disseminating sex knowledge, without morality, to their children in school." In Levittown, New York, the election in 1956 of a new public school board, a majority of whose members were Catholic, resulted in the immediate cancellation of the exhibition of a film on menstruation for the girl students. In these and similar cases the Church does not dispute the desirability and even necessity of proper sex education of the young. It takes the position, however, that this is the exclusive and sacred responsibility of the family, aided by the family's spiritual advisers.

In this respect the position of the Catholic Church must be distinguished from that of the Christian Science Church. Christian Scientists object to the compulsory participation of their children in the public schools in instruction on the germ theory of disease, a theory inconsistent with Christian Science teachings. They do not, however, object to the inclusion of such teaching in the public school curriculum so long as their children are excused from participating. (On the other hand, it must be pointed out that the Christian Science Church vigorously opposes fluoridation of municipal water supplies even though the majority of the residents are not Christian Scientists and have no conscientious objections to drinking fluoridated water.)

The Catholic position is closer to that of the Jewish organizations, which are not content with having Jewish children excused from religious instruction in the public schools but demand that the schools abstain from giving such instruction to any children. Since the Jewish organizations (like the Protestant) do not oppose sex education in the public schools, but on the contrary resent Catholic efforts to eliminate it, a charge of inconsistency might be leveled against them.

Nevertheless, a real and valid distinction exists between the two situations. Sex education (or germ theory education) is a secular endeavor properly within the scope of activities of a secular school system. If participation in sex education (or germ theory education) violates the conscience of some of the children or their parents, the requirements of religious liberty may entitle these children to absent themselves from the instruction, but it does not entitle them to deprive other willing children from participating. Religious instruction, however, is an entirely different matter. Here the question is not one of the religious liberty of a minority but the right of a secular school conducted and controlled by a secular state to intrude upon the area of religion. Under our constitutional system of the separation of church and state, it would be illegal and unconstitutional for a public school to teach religion even if all the parents of all the children consented to it.

DIVORCE

Protestants, Catholics, and Jews are agreed that the widespread prevalence of divorce in the United States represents a grave problem. They agree too that the state of divorce laws and civil divorce procedures is shocking and deplorable. They agree further that the situation cries desperately for remedial action. But at this point their agreement ends. There is a wide difference among them, principally between the Catholics and non-Catholics, as to the cause of the evil and the nature of the appropriate remedial action.

The situation in New York dramatically illustrates the problem and the division. The law of the state permits divorce on only one ground, adultery. Yet it is well known (and has been substantiated by an investigation conducted in New York City in 1948) that divorce can easily be obtained in New York if both parties are willing and are not squeamish about committing a little perjury. The effect, therefore, is that, for all practical purposes, divorce is obtainable in New York on no ground at all other than mutual consent; the only price the parties need pay (besides counsel and court fees) is a slight lowering of their standards of honesty and truthfulness.

To many non-Catholics the solution must include (although, of course, not be limited to) recognizing reality by amending the divorce laws to allow other grounds for divorce, such as desertion, cruelty, etc. To the Catholic Church, however, the obvious answer is the reverse: not to liberalize divorce laws and procedures but to tighten and strengthen them. So determined is the opposition of the Catholic Church to liberalized divorce, and so strong is its influence in New York, that there is hardly a chance that the New York divorce statute will be liberalized in the immediate future. Indeed, it is difficult to find a legislator who is willing to introduce a bill for liberalized divorce.

The Catholic Church in New York opposes even legislative inquiries and studies of the divorce laws and their operation, lest such studies lead to liberalizing legislation. For years efforts have been made in the New York State legislature to establish study commissions. In 1955 a rural district Republican Assemblywoman, Janet Hill Gordon, who for years had been introducing such bills without success, was joined by a rural district Republican state senator, who was also a Methodist clergyman, Dutton S. Peterson, in sponsoring a bill to establish a temporary state commission to study New York's marriage and divorce laws. The measure was warmly supported by the (Protestant) State Council of Churches and the New York (Jewish) Board of Rabbis. It was opposed by the State Roman Catholic Welfare Committee, whose representatives characterized the measure as the "entering wedge of a drive for liberalization of the law," and urged instead the enactment of measures aimed at the "preservation of the marital relationship and the family unit," as for example by establishing mandatory conciliation facilities for divorce applicants and restricting actions for annulment. Neither the Gordon-Peterson measure nor the Catholic Church-sponsored measure (opposed by the Protestant-Jewish-secular humanist alliance) succeeded of passage.

Catholic opposition to liberalizing the divorce laws is difficult to justify, even within the terms of Catholic dogma and principles. Contraceptive birth control, artificial insemination, and abortion are all violations of natural law and forbidden to all human beings. But Catholicism does not deny that divorce is permissible under the law of Moses or Mohammed; Jesus forbade divorce only to those who entered into the holy sacrament of marriage. The Church's opposition to a liberalized divorce procedure permissible to non-Christians is therefore much like Protestant (and now also Catholic) opposition to liberalizing compulsory Sabbath-observance laws. The liberalization of secular laws, it is feared, will tend to make Christians lax in observing the religious obligations of their faith, and Catholicism is no more averse today than Protestantism was formerly to employing governmental sanctions to fortify its own religious efforts. Here again is reflected the urge of religious groups to translate their own concepts and values into imperatives for the entire community.

CHILD WELFARE

Religious bodies have had a long and honorable history in the upbringing and welfare of children. Few ethical commands of the Bible are emphasized more than the duty of protecting the fatherless. The Talmud lists support and education of the orphan as one of the principal obligations of charity. Christianity, by its dogma of individual salvation through grace and redemption, greatly softened the Roman concept of parental hegemony and laid the foundation for modern principles of child welfare. The Catholic dogma of the equal sanctity of mother and unborn child, while, as we have seen, completely unacceptable to non-Catholics, nevertheless shows the importance of children in the Catholic religion.

From its very beginning, the Christian church undertook the responsibility of caring for orphans and foundlings. With the legal recognition of Christianity under Constantine in the fourth century, church institutions for orphans and others in need became widespread throughout the empire, and church responsibility in this area continued through the Middle Ages. In this country religious groups were the first to enter the field of child welfare. The first private orphan asylum in America was established by the Ursuline Convent in New Orleans in the early eighteenth century. Today, the majority of institutions in the United States caring for children are operated by religious groups.

At this point it may be timely to remind the reader again that the statements made in this book are usually generalizations, that it is in the nature of generalizations to have exceptions, qualifications, and modifications, but that generalizations may nevertheless be valid and that most of life's decisions must be based upon them. Certainly in the area covered in these pages generalizations have tremendous practical consequences.

With this caveat in mind, it may be suggested that the Catholic Church scrutinizes with suspicion, if not hostility, any legislation seeking to regulate child welfare. There are a number of contributing causes for this attitude, all reflecting Catholic dogma, principles, and values. One is the general antipathy of the Church to any legislation seeking to regulate family relationships, legislation that, in the eyes of the Church, is presumptively an infringement upon familial sovereignty. Another is the theological premise that religion is more important than considerations of secular or temporal welfare in the upbringing of children, and state regulation by its nature generally concerns itself exclusively with considerations of temporal welfare. A third factor is Catholic questioning as to whether the state has any right to operate welfare institutions at all. From the time of the Council of Trent, the predominant view in Catholicism has been that all charitable work, including the upbringing and welfare of children, is a function of the Church.

For these reasons the Church is suspicious of social welfare legislation that goes beyond the granting of funds to families. (This it strongly favors.) It urges the contraction and eventual disappearance of public (i.e., governmental) welfare institutions, particularly those concerned with children, and the corresponding expansion of denominational institutions supported by tax-raised funds. It sees little justification for secular welfare institutions, and urges that a child who has become the ward of the state should be assigned to a denominational institution of the same faith. Such a procedure would be consistent with Catholic theory that tends to classify all persons under some religious category.

Catholic child welfare agencies are conducted exclusively under church auspices to the same extent as Catholic hospitals and Catholic schools. Catholic philosophy looks to education and the upbringing of children as preparation for Catholic life, which is itself but a preparation for eternal salvation. It is natural, therefore, that temporal welfare considerations are to be subordinated to eternal welfare considerations in all matters affecting children, as in all other cases.

Neither Protestantism nor Judaism views social welfare legislation with the immanent antipathy of the Catholic Church. On the contrary, the social gospel has become a dominant aspect of much of American Protestantism and Judaism. In Protestant and Jewish welfare institutions, temporal considerations play a more significant role and religious considerations a less significant role than in Catholic institutions. The Protestant agencies vary in the closeness of their affinity to Protestant church bodies. In most cases there is a large degree of lay control, and temporal considerations are no less weighty than religious. Among Jewish welfare agencies the emphasis upon non-sectarian considerations is even greater. Jewish social work is not synagogue-centered but community-centered, and more and more Jewish-controlled welfare agencies are operated as non-sectarian institutions. (One of the chief reasons for this development is the rapid economic rise of the Jewish community in America, with the consequence that in the great majority of communities there are simply not enough needy Jews who qualify for philanthropic aid.) For these and other reasons one finds little opposition among Protestant and Jewish religious groups either to state operation of welfare institutions or to state supervision of private and denominational welfare institutions.

In the area of juvenile delinquency another generalization may be risked. Catholicism looks at juvenile delinquency as a problem in discipline, Protestantism and Judaism (and, of course, secular humanism) as a problem in child welfare. The Catholic emphasis is upon the upholding of authority and the moral code; the Protestant-Jewish emphasis is upon the child in trouble. In handling the child, Catholicism is more likely to emphasize the need for punishment.

It is also most insistent upon involvement of church and religion. If the child is placed on probation, the Church is more likely to insist that the probation officer be of the same religious faith as the child, that the co-operation of church and church agencies be enlisted, and that religious training be made part of the treatment decreed by the children's court.

ADOPTION

The issues and divisions in the field of interreligious adoptions and custody contests can perhaps be best indicated by recounting three of the many cases that have recently reached the courts, two occurring in Massachusetts and one in Pennsylvania. All three attracted nation-wide attention and dramatized the competing value judgments among the major faiths.

The first, the Goldman case, involved twins born out of wedlock to a Catholic mother, who, being unable to care for them, gave them to the Goldmans, a childless Jewish couple in Lynn, Massachusetts, to be raised as their children. When the couple had had the twins for three years, they presented to the appropriate court a petition for their legal adoption. The twins' mother signed an affidavit in which she stated that she consented to the adoption, knowing that the couple were Jewish and would bring up the twins as Jews. The judge, although he found that the couple were in all respects fit and proper and would give the twins parental affection and a good home, nevertheless refused to allow the adoption because of the difference in religions. He ruled that even though the twins had never been baptized, they were Catholic since they had been born to a Catholic mother.

The ruling was affirmed by the highest court in Massachusetts, and the United States Supreme Court refused to review the decision, although probably on technical grounds. After the legal proceedings were ended, the Massachusetts Department of Public Welfare sought to compel the Goldmans to surrender the twins so that they might be placed in a Catholic institution. The Goldmans, upon hearing of the Department's intentions, abandoned their home, business, and non-mobile assets and departed with the twins to establish a new home in another state. The Department indicated that it would not let the matter drop but would seek to extradite the Goldmans and thus recover the twins so that they might be placed in a Catholic institution. Apparently, however, it was unable to trace the Goldmans or the twins, who presumably are today living together somewhere as a family unit.

The second, the even more publicized "Hildy" case, was substantially the same as the Goldmans' with one exception; in this instance the unmarried Catholic mother of the child claimed that she did not know that the Ellises, to whom she gave the child for adoption, were Jewish and that as soon as she found out, she sought to recover the child so that it could be placed in a Catholic institution. The Catholic Church has made much of this fact. It has been particularly bitter about the Jewish community's silence about the case in view of its vigorous defense of the Jewish aunt in the Finaly case in France in her efforts to recover two Jewish boys who had been placed in the custody of the mistress of a Catholic nursery when their parents were taken by the Nazi occupation forces to an extermination camp in the East.

Yet it is important to note that the mother's change of mind in the Hildy case was not of any legal significance nor was it considered a vital factor by the Church. In the Goldman case the mother did not change her mind but throughout approved the adoption of her twins by the Jewish couple. Nevertheless, the law of Massachusetts would not allow it. The Church vigorously fought the adoption in the Goldman case and there is no reason to believe that it would have been less vigorous in its opposition in the Hildy case even if the mother had not changed her mind.

As in the Goldman case, the Massachusetts child welfare authorities sought to recover the child for placement in a Catholic institution. This time they were successful in locating the Jewish couple, who had moved to Florida, and instituted extradition proceedings against them, charging them with the crime of kidnaping. The extradition was supported by all organs of the Catholic Church, within and without Massachusetts; it was opposed by Protestant organizations, clergymen, and publications, within and without Massachusetts; and the Jewish community maintained a discreet silence. The governor of Florida refused the extradition, and a Florida court later allowed the adoption that had been refused by the Massachusetts courts.

The third case was decided in the courts of Pennsylvania. The crazed neighbor of a young couple in Michigan entered their house and shot them both. The husband had been a Catholic; the wife a Protestant. They had one young child whom they had agreed to rear in the Catholic faith and accordingly had had him baptized as a Catholic. On the death of the couple, the child's (Protestant) maternal aunt came from Pennsylvania, took him and brought him back with her with the intent to adopt him. The child's (Catholic) paternal grandparents followed her to Pennsylvania, and, with the support and backing of the Catholic Church, brought legal proceedings to recover the child for adoption by them. The Pennsylvania courts ruled in favor of the aunt and her husband on the ground that the welfare of the child dictated that he be brought up away from the scene of the tragedy and by a couple whose age relationship to him was more nearly that of the normal age relationship between parents and children. While the religious factor, the court said, is important and must be given consideration, it may not be allowed to override the demands of the child's welfare.

These cases are typical rather than unique; similar cases are reaching the courts with increasing frequency. They are difficult cases and almost invariably give rise to interreligious tensions and acrimony. They are difficult because they involve a number of conflicting claims, all of which appear just and reasonable. There is first the child's claim to a normal family life with adoptive parents who are able and anxious to give it security, affection, and an opportunity for happiness. There is the claim of the would-be parents themselves, usually a childless couple desperately seeking a child upon whom they can lavish their affection. There is the claim of the natural mother who wants the child to have the happiness she herself is unable to provide, but who also wants it to be raised in her own faith—wishes that sometimes are mutually exclusive. And finally, there is the claim of the church or religious group to the allegiance of the mother and child.

In a number of states the legislatures have sought to adjust these conflicting claims by providing that "where practicable" children should be adopted by couples of the same religious persuasion as the natural parents. Until recently the courts have almost uniformly construed these so-called "religious protection" laws, as the Pennsylvania courts did in the case recounted above, not as prohibiting all interreligious adoptions but only as requiring consideration of religion as one of the factors in determining whether or not an adoption should be approved. If, for example, the choice is between two couples, each of good character and each able to provide the child with a good home, security, and affection, preference would be given to the couple having the same religion as the child's parents. If, on the other hand, the choice is between a normal family life and an institution, the courts would approve the adoption notwithstanding religious differences, particularly if the natural parent consents to the adoption, but also if by reason of the natural parent's death or disappearance, her consent cannot be obtained.

This was the law even in Massachusetts before the Goldman case. Shortly before that case reached the courts, Massachusetts allowed a Protestant couple to adopt a child born to a Catholic mother. The decision was bitterly criticized by the Boston *Pilot*. The *Pilot* explained the deep anxiety of the Church because "for Catholics their faith is their most treasured possession," and it is therefore "small wonder that they would wish to see it passed on to the coming generation as their road to salvation as well." The decision in the Goldman case, which in effect closed the Massachusetts courts to interreligious adoptions, made it unnecessary for the Church to seek amendment of the statutes of that state, but it has undertaken a nation-wide campaign to amend adoption laws in other states in order to bar interreligious adoptions. That the Church has had some success in the legislatures can be seen from the following story which appeared in the *Tablet*, organ of the Brooklyn Diocese:

A new [Pennsylvania] State child adoption bill was passed by the legislature and sent to Gov. John S. Fine for signature after a Senate-House conference had amended the measure to eliminate features condemned—and include others advocated—by Pennsylvania Catholic leaders. Two other bills sponsored, as was the child adoption measure, by the Governor's Committee on Children and Youth and backed by civil, welfare and some Protestant church groups [1] *were killed in the House after a plea by Archbishop John F. O'Hara of Philadelphia and Catholic Bishops throughout the State brought a flood of protests to the capital.*

The success of the Church in overcoming Protestant-humanist opposition is in part attributable to the ambivalence of non-Catholic social welfare agencies concerned with adoption. Agencies whose sole or primary concern is the welfare and happiness of children are not likely to relish sacrificing that objective and are therefore generally opposed to "religious protection" laws that would make reli-

[1] Note the Protestant-humanist alliance.

gious identity the determinative criterion in adoptions. On the other hand, to meet the serious evils of the "black market" in babies, the agencies have been pressing for laws imposing stricter regulation on adoptions. To obtain Catholic Church support for such laws the agencies must frequently pay the price of agreeing to strict "religious protection" provisions.

The position of the Catholic Church is quite logical and understandable in the light of its dogmatic concepts and philosophical principles. Those particularly relevant here are that (a) religion is a matter of status and not of election; (b) Catholic baptism is immutable and accordingly there is no exit from the Catholic faith; (c) eternal salvation is more important than temporal happiness, and if a choice must be made the first must always be chosen above the second; (d) Catholicism is the one and only true faith, and membership therein is the surest if not the only certain road to eternal salvation; (e) voluntariness is not the ultimate test nor basic requirement in religion, and therefore the wishes of a Catholic mother that her child be adopted by a couple of a non-Catholic faith need not be honored (". . . no one," said a Catholic judge in a Massachusetts custody case, "not even the parents have the right to deny an immature child who has been baptized a Roman Catholic the privilege of being reared in Catholicity"); (f) the Church has a legitimate and legally recognizable interest in the faith of its members and has the right to call upon the state to use its machinery to protect that interest and preserve the sovereignty of the Church over its members.

None of these concepts or principles is acceptable either to Protestantism or to secular humanism, and it was therefore no more than to be expected that the Catholic position is strenuously contested by the Protestant-humanist alliance. In the Hildy case, the Massachusetts Council of Churches urged the Florida governor to base his decision in the extradition primarily on the welfare of the child. Methodist Bishop John Wesley Lord of Boston asserted that superior to the Massachusetts law was "moral judgment [which] must always be the last judgment in any matter." "It is," he continued, "moral judgment that, for the welfare and good of this six-year-old adopted daughter, the law be superseded by the divine law of love. . . . This devout Jewish people, at sacrifice of earthly possessions and with a devotion none can deny, wishes to continue to rear the child in a home in which love and devotion are the paramount factors. No law of the land can supersede moral law." In Missouri, the local chapter of Protestants and Other Americans United for Separation of Church and State joined with the local chapter of the American Civil Liberties Union and the local chapter of the American Jewish Congress to oppose a bill that sought to add a "religious protection" clause to the state's adoption law.

Despite this action of the local chapter of the American Jewish Congress and despite the intervention of the American Jewish Congress in the Goldman case on behalf of the Goldmans, it cannot be said that at the time of this writing there is a crystallized Jewish position on the subject of interreligious adoptions. (The American Jewish Congress is a civic, not a religious, organization.) The dogmatic concepts of Judaism are in some aspects similar to, or identical with, those of Roman Catholicism. According to traditional Jewish concepts religion is a matter of status which is inherited through the mother. Traditional Judaism, no less than Catholicism, recognizes no complete exit from the faith. While even Orthodox Judaism asserts that "the righteous of all nations have a share in Kingdom Come," there is within Judaism an instinctive, emotional, and almost irrational repugnance to the thought of a Jewish-born child being raised in a non-Jewish faith.

On the other side is the cordial relationship between American Judaism and the Protestant-humanist alliance and sympathy with its principles and concepts. It is this ambivalence, and not the fact that the Goldsmans and Ellises were Jewish, that explains the silence of the Jewish religious organizations, rabbinic and congregational, in the Goldman and Hildy cases. It cannot safely be predicted at this time what position American Judaism will ultimately take on the question of interreligious adoptions, or if indeed there will ever be a sufficient degree of unanimity within Judaism to arrive at a common position. Nevertheless, the fact that in June, 1957, the New York Board of Rabbis joined the American Jewish Congress in urging a New York State Constitutional Committee that the state constitution be amended to make it clear that interreligious adoptions will be allowed where consistent with the welfare of the child and the wishes of the natural parents, would seem to indicate that here too the effects of cultural competition upon the principles, concepts, and development of religious groups are beginning to take effect and that here too American Judaism will ultimately find itself in the camp of its natural allies, Protestant dissent and secular humanism.

8. ISSUES DOMESTIC AND FOREIGN

THE SOCIAL GOSPEL

All three major faiths are neck deep in political action. The National Catholic Welfare Conference maintains its office in Washington and its representatives keep in close and continuous contact with affairs at the Capitol. While none of the Jewish religious bodies and few of the Protestant denominations maintain full-time professional legislative representatives to press their organization's particular views in the legislative lobbies (the Quakers and perhaps the Baptists are exceptions), all of them issue formal pronouncements on a variety of public issues and make certain that the occupants of both the Capitol and the White House and the corresponding houses in the states are kept informed of these views.

All three major faiths express interest and take political action in some areas of what has been called the social gospel, i.e., issues of social and economic significance not narrowly religious. On some issues the three faiths have substantially common objectives. They are opposed to racial segregation and committed to effectuation of the decisions of the United States Supreme Court requiring racial integration in the public schools. They are opposed to racial discrimination and look favorably upon laws prohibiting discrimination. They are dissatisfied with our present immigration laws and urge liberalization aimed at allowing larger numbers of immigrants and particularly refugees to enter the country.

On the whole, however, it may be said that while the Catholic Church is more active politically in public issues closely related to religion and church, it is less concerned than Protestantism or Judaism with those of primary social and economic significance. (That Catholic—and Jewish—Representatives and Senators are generally liberal on these issues is most reasonably explained by the fact that they usually represent urban areas.) There are at least two reasons for this, both consistent with the hypotheses suggested in this book. In the first place, as has been noted elsewhere, Catholicism is an other-world religion whose primary concern is with eternal salvation rather than temporal happiness. (Earlier German Catholics in the Midwest, acting principally through the Central-Verein, sought to create a pattern of social action, but their efforts failed with the emergent dominance of the east coast Irish Catholicism and its Roman-trained prelates.) In the second place, American Catholicism has far less than Protestantism or Judaism adjusted itself to the values of secular humanism.

Even in those areas of the social gospel in which the Catholic Church takes an active interest, it is reluctant to work jointly with the other faiths. Catholic clerics rarely join with Protestant and Jewish clerics, and Catholic organizations rarely join with Protestant and Jewish organizations in joint statements, preferring to issue parallel but independent statements. (There are exceptions to this in some localities, and particularly in respect to issues in which the Catholic Church takes a primary interest, such as the anti-obscenity or anti-Sabbath desecration campaigns.) This reluctance is based upon the desire of the Church to avoid any conduct that might give rise to the impression that it accepts the equality of religions as well as by its related desire to channel all activities of the faithful exclusively through the Church.

American Protestantism has a long tradition of involvement in social and political issues. At the birth of our nation, the clergy took an active and articulate role on one side or the other in the struggle for independence. Later it was the Protestant clergy that spearheaded the Abolitionist movement. The crusade against intoxicating liquors was almost exclusively a Protestant church endeavor. Protestant clergymen often took the lead in campaigns against municipal corruption. During the period of the great depression in the nineteen-thirties, and of World War II in the forties, the Federal Council of Churches issued many proclamations on social, economic, and political issues. The merger of the Federal Council into the National Council of Churches, the general prosperity of the nation and the "religious revival" of the fifties have resulted in a substantial lessening in the number of pan-Protestant official statements on social and economic issues, but the constituent denominations still make their voices heard.

Of the three major faiths, American Judaism is most concerned with the social gospel. One need but glance through a biography of Rabbi Stephen Wise to get an idea of the variety of social and economic issues in which this typical American Reform rabbi took an active interest. At one time or another, the Central Conference of American Rabbis (Reform) has taken positions and issued public pronouncements on such social and economic problems as industrial democracy, the right of unionization, unemployment, working conditions, child labor, lynching, immigration, Federal aid to public schools, public housing, and a variety of similar problems. A book entitled *Justice and Judaism* by Vorspan and Lipman, published in 1956 by the Union of American Hebrew Congregations (Reform), gives an idea of the great range of social issues that are deemed by the Reform wing of American Judaism to be the proper concern of synagogues.

While the Conservative and Orthodox wings of American Judaism do not have the same comprehensive background in the social gospel, both are rapidly expanding their activities in this area. This trend is likely to be accelerated and intensified by the movement to the suburbs—particularly noticeable among Jews—which results in the centralization of activities through the communal synagogue. The fact that the Reform rabbinate, which has always represented the higher economic classes in the Jewish community, has been the most active and the most liberal in the social gospel field, would seem to indicate that the rapid economic rise of the Jewish community is not likely to exercise a significant retarding influence on this trend.

Protestant and Jewish religious organizations are quite eager to work jointly and co-operatively toward the achievement of the many social objectives they share. They are also eager to co-operate with Catholic organizations toward these ends. While they generally understand the reasons for the reluctance of Catholic clerics to join in co-operative interfaith movements for social advancement, it cannot be fairly said that they accept these reasons as valid or that they indicate any real sympathetic appreciation for the position or motivations of the Catholic Church.

Yet here too the effects of cultural competition are at work. There is a slow but clearly discernible liberalization of the Catholic attitude toward interfaith co-operation in political and civic action for the achievement of common goals. I have earlier mentioned the leadership taken by Catholic priests and organizations in co-operative efforts against obscenity and Sabbath desecration. In the field of immigration reform one can find substantial Catholic co-operation in joint ventures that include Protestant, Jewish, and secular organizations. To some extent this is also to be found in efforts toward racial integration. Barring some unforeseen turn of events, it is reasonably safe to predict that this trend will continue and expand.

COMMUNISM WITHIN THE GATES

American Catholicism, far more than either Protestantism or Judaism, is concerned with the menace of domestic communism. If one scans the news and editorial pages of the Catholic press throughout the nation, one will get an idea of the degree and extent of Catholic concern. For the past decade Catholicism has considered American communism the most important issue on the domestic scene, just as it considers Soviet communism the most important issue on the foreign scene.

During the brief period of his power Senator Joseph R. McCarthy's most ardent and passionate support came from the Catholic Church and the Catholic community. Even after he was discredited and had sunk back into political obscurity, McCarthy remained a hero, probably the number one national hero, in the eyes of American Catholicism. Upon his death the Catholic press was uniformly eulogistic in its editorial comment. The *Catholic Review* of Baltimore stated that "Senator McCarthy was attempting to do a job he and every other right-thinking American knew had to be done." *Tidings* of Los Angeles said that he "threw himself across the barbed wire of the Communist positions that others could advance and attack their entrenched place in American life." The *Florida Catholic* called him an "illustrious soldier, Senator and Christian patriot." The *Catholic News* of New York, organ of Cardinal Spellman, expressed regret that "Canada and England did not have a Joe McCarthy to shock them out of their complacency on Communism." The *Register Times-Review* of La Crosse, Wisconsin, summed up the causes of McCarthy's decline and death briefly: "Any prominent figure who dares to be courageous and fearless in fighting Communism will be crucified and crushed." (I suggest that there may be some psychological significance in the use of the word "crucified.")

These are typical of the comments that appeared in the Catholic press on McCarthy's death. In a few of the publications there could be found apology for, and disagreement with, some of the methods used by the late Senator, but the only real dissent came from *Commonweal*. However, as has been pointed out earlier, this lay-controlled magazine is frequently at odds with the Hierarchy and has little significant influence within the Catholic Church.

Occasionally American Catholicism, to its embarrassment, finds itself more anti-Communist than the Vatican. When reports reached America that the Pope had expressed the hope that President Eisenhower would extend clemency to Julius and Ethel Rosenberg, the Communists who had been sentenced to death for turning over atomic secrets to the Soviet government, the Catholic press first vigorously denied the reports and then went to great efforts to explain the Pope's action and minimize its significance.

The intensity of Catholic opposition to communism is hardly surprising. The philosophy and objectives of communism and those of Catholicism are completely antithetical. Historically Roman Catholicism has always been hostile to revolutionary movements, and the Vatican was from the beginning unfriendly to the Russian Revolution as it had a century and a quarter earlier been unfriendly to the French Revolution. International Catholicism and international communism were always bitter enemies, an enmity intensified by the Spanish Civil War.

Nevertheless, I submit, this is not the whole explanation. It does not adequately explain why American Catholicism should at times be more anti-Communist than the Pope nor why millions of Catholics in Italy and other European countries find it possible to go from mass and confession to the polling places to vote the Communist party ticket or to their union polling booth to vote for avowed Communists as their shop stewards and union officers.

Again I suggest that some of the explanation lies in terms of cultural competition. The only group in America that rivals the Catholic Church in its anti-Communist feelings are the extreme nationalists—the American Legion and other veterans groups. American Catholicism's intense enmity to communism is likewise a manifestation of its extreme nationalism. Of the religious faiths in America, Catholicism is easily the most nationalistic. At first glance this seems surprising, for American Catholicism is part of the most international of all religions. But while there is much in Catholic dogma and concepts that makes impossible or difficult American Catholicism's adjustment to secular-humanist values in American culture, nothing prevents its adjustment to nationalist values in American culture. Catholicism's anti-communism and extreme nationalism are, it seems to me, in part motivated by the same factors that motivate its anti-obscenity and Sabbath observance crusades.

Partly because American Judaism has adjusted happily to the secular-humanist elements in American culture, partly because of its tradition of radicalism going back to the first generation of Jewish immigrants from eastern Europe in the late nineteenth and early twentieth centuries, partly because of the prophetic tradition which inclines Judaism sympathetically to any cause that purports to speak in the name of justice, and partly for other reasons one does not find within Judaism any such widespread and passionate hatred of communism and Communists as is found in Catholicism. Among the signatories to petitions for clemency for the Rosenbergs there were proportionately a far greater number of rabbis than of Protestant clergymen. (Catholic priests were, of course, conspicuously absent.)

During the period of intense anti-Communist feeling, a major network required all its broadcasters to sign oaths to the effect that they were not Communists. A noted news commentator refused to sign the oath, stating that he was a devout Roman Catholic and therefore could not be a Communist. (The company accepted this explanation and did not press the matter.) During the same period it was reliably reported that in the course of screening Federal employees to expel Communists from government service a letter from a Catholic priest to the effect that the particular employee was a communicant of his church served without more ado to establish the employee's non-communism. A similar letter from a rabbi had no such effect. Within the Jewish community this report aroused a considerable sense of unjust and discriminatory treatment. Yet this apparent discrimination was hardly an unrealistic appraisal of the actual situation. In any event, it is certain that proportionate to their numbers there was a much greater number of Jews than non-Jews in the ranks of American communism.

In the degree of its opposition to communism and its hostility to Communists, American Protestantism stands closer to Judaism than to Catholicism. (It must be remembered that throughout this book the term "Protestantism" is used to indicate the pan-Protestantism represented by the National Council of Churches, and not the Fundamentalist Protestantism represented by the American Council of Churches, just as the term "Judaism" is used to indicate the pan-Judaism represented by the Synagogue Council of America and not the small extreme Orthodox wing.) In 1958, a bill to extend the life of the Massachusetts Commission on Communism was endorsed by representatives of the Catholic Church and opposed by Protestant and Jewish spokesmen. A Methodist bishop, G. Bromley Oxnam, was questioned by a Congressional committee as to his loyalty and his alleged sympathy for Communist causes. Lesser-known Protestant clergymen were also subject to Congressional committees on communism and un-American activities. One chairman of the House Committee on Un-American Activities went so far as to announce the launching of an investigation on communism within the churches, and it was no secret that what he had in mind were the Protestant churches. Such treatment of Catholic bishops, priests, or churches would have been inconceivable.

This difference in treatment is explained by the difference in the degree of opposition to communism and hatred of Communists between Catholicism on the one hand and Protestantism and Judaism on the other. Neither Protestantism nor Judaism was part of an international church that was the world's foremost opponent of Soviet and international communism. Protestantism had been spared much of the persecution and oppression suffered by that part of eastern Europe that came under Soviet domination. Moreover, the very intensity of Catholic anti-communism may well have had a negative effect upon the Protestant clergy, many of whom considered communism and Catholicism almost equally undesirable totalitarianisms. Finally, there was within Protestantism a substantial segment that sympathized with the goal, though not the methods, of the Communist experiment. The "Red Dean" of Canterbury had his counterparts in America; a "Red Dean" in Catholicism is unthinkable. In any event, prior to the onset of the "cold war," many Protestant ministers and Jewish rabbis were members of, or co-operated with, organizations which were dominated by Communists or in which Communists took an active part. No Catholic priests could be found in these organizations. (It need hardly be said that on the whole both

Protestantism and Judaism are and always have been opposed to communism. The difference is that with Catholicism, anti-communism was always an overriding consideration precluding any contact with Communists, while with many Protestant and Jewish clergymen anti-communism could be subordinated to the achievement of a common goal, such as peace or elimination of racial discrimination.)

CIVIL LIBERTIES

Catholic concern with the dangers of domestic communism is matched by Jewish concern with encroachments upon civil liberties. A Catholic priest reading about a proposed investigation of subversion in government, in the press, or in the entertainment industry, is likely to think first of the danger of communism; a rabbi reading the same press report is likely to think first of civil liberties. To the priest, the threat of communism is the overriding consideration. If that threat can be opposed effectively within the framework of civil liberties, well and good. If it cannot, then civil liberties must yield to the more important end. To the rabbi the more immediate danger is likely to be the threat to civil liberties. And just as the priest is likely to think that the rabbi naïvely underestimates the danger of domestic communism, the rabbi is likely to think that the priest hysterically overestimates it.

It cannot be said that Judaism's devotion to civil liberties is as intense and as passionate as Catholicism's hatred of communism. Should Judaism be faced with the unavoidable choice of a Communist America or extreme restrictions on civil liberties, there is not the slightest doubt that it would choose the latter as the lesser evil. But Judaism does not believe America is now or is likely in the predictable future to be faced with that choice. It is convinced that the threat of communism can be adequately dealt with within the framework of traditional American liberties, and while it recognizes that this approach carries with it some risk, it believes that absolute security is in any event not attainable and that some risks can and should be taken.

The difference in approach to civil liberties between Judaism and Catholicism is quite understandable. In its accommodation to the secular-humanist ethic in America, Judaism has accepted its basic premise of the innate goodness of man and the assumption that given free choice man will choose good rather than evil, right rather than wrong, and freedom rather than despotism. Hence, Judaism is convinced that given free and open discussion of all points of view and given free choice, the American people can be relied upon to choose the democratic way of life, and that when the government in meeting the problem of domestic communism is faced with a choice between liberty and security it is safer to err on the side of liberty.

Catholicism proceeds from a directly opposite premise. Secular humanism has had little influence upon American Catholicism as a whole and even less upon the basic Catholic premise of the innate fallibility and wickedness of man. Original sin looms as large in Catholic theology today as it ever did. Unless guided by wiser leadership, in church and state, man cannot be counted on to know the right way, and unless restrained and disciplined by higher authority, in church and state, man cannot be counted on to choose the right way even after it is pointed out to him.

It is quite natural, therefore, that proposals for ever wider investigations of subversive activities, for tightening of security laws, for restrictions on use of the Fifth Amendment privilege against self-incrimination, for compelling ex-Communists to inform upon their former associates, or a variety of similar proposals should be warmly supported by the Catholic press and organizations, and that they should be met with suspicion, antipathy, or active opposition by Jewish organizations. It is quite natural too that the reverence which American Catholicism accorded Senator McCarthy was matched by the reverence accorded by American Judaism to Senator Herbert H. Lehman, the foremost champion of civil liberties in Congress during the height of McCarthy's domination of the American political scene. The fact that Lehman is a Jew and McCarthy was a Catholic, while significant in the terms of my thesis, does not explain this almost universal Jewish respect for Lehman and extreme dislike for McCarthy, as is evidenced by the fact that McCarthy's unpopularity within the Jewish community was not less than that of his two Jewish disciples, Roy Cohn and Rabbi Benjamin Shultz.

Judaism's concern with civil liberties is on the whole shared by Protestantism (again, disregarding the extreme Fundamentalist wing). Completely independent of the influence of secular humanism, and probably more important, is the long libertarian tradition of Protestant dissent. At the time our Constitution was written, Protestant dissent was as ardent a supporter of a bill of rights as Jeffersonian humanism. Protestant dissent was no less committed to the social-contract theory and the concept of governmental powers strictly limited to those delegated to it by the people, and was no less suspicious of a strong government. Moreover, the basic Protestant assumption that every man has the capacity to read and understand the Bible and to commune with God is naturally conducive to a libertarian approach in the political arena.

For these and other reasons Protestantism is in the forefront of the struggle to preserve civil liberties. During the McCarthy era the voices of Protestant leaders such as G. Bromley Oxnam, John A. Mackay, and Eugene Carson Blake could be heard even above the voices of Jewish religious leaders. (The reasons for this are that there are far more Protestant than Jewish clergymen, and that Protestantism was, or felt itself, less vulnerable to charges of pro-Communist sympathies and therefore had greater freedom to say publicly what it believed privately.) Here, as in so many other areas of public concern, the alliance of Protestantism, Judaism, and secular humanism (e.g., the American Civil Liberties Union) holds fast.

WAR, PEACE, PACIFICISM, AND THE ATOM BOMB

Of the three major faiths, Protestantism has been the most vocal and active in support of peace movements. The Church Peace Union and a number of similar organizations were organized under Protestant sponsorship to promote the cause of world peace. In 1934 a questionnaire sent to some 100,000 Protestant clergymen, and returned by about one-fifth of the recipients, revealed that two-thirds of those who answered believed that the churches should not sanction or support any future war, and about the same number stated that as individuals they would not participate in or sanction any future war. Only one-third felt that there was a sufficient moral distinction between "aggressive" and "defensive" wars to justify sanction or support of the latter.

The spread of Nazi domination over Europe and the outbreak of World War II effected a substantial change in Protantism on the issue of war and peace. Yet, up to the day of Pearl Harbor, *The Christian Century*, the nation's leading Protestant publication, vigorously opposed American entry into the war or even the rendering of such aid to Great Britain as carried with it the risk of American involvement. The American Protestant clergy was split down the middle on the issue. A strong minority favored completely *The Christian Century's* position. Another strong minority favored all-out intervention on the side of Great Britain. (*Christianity and Crisis* was launched under the editorship of Reinhold Niebuhr as an organ for the views of this segment of Protestantism.) The majority of Protestant clergymen were probably in the center, favoring material aid to Britain but shunning direct involvement in the war.

Pearl Harbor effectively stilled Protestant opposition to war and to the particular war in which America was engaged. In 1940 the Methodist General Conference asserted unequivocally and unqualifiedly that "the Methodist Church . . . will not officially endorse, support or participate in war." Four years later it adopted a resolution which "in Christ's name" invoked "the blessing of God upon the men in the armed forces," prayed "for victory," and declared that it is "well within the Christian position" to assert "the necessity of the use of military force to resist an aggression which would overthrow every right which is held sacred by civilized men." Yet it is significant that the clergy in the Conference were almost exactly divided on the resolution, which carried only because of the two to one vote in its favor on the part of the laity in the Conference. (The resolution was bitterly denounced by *The Christian Century*.)

The return of peace revived the strong pro-pacificism of American Protestantism. Today the Protestant clergy is again taking the lead in the call for the complete and total abolition of war. Even proportionately, more Protestant clergymen signed the Stockholm Peace Petition than clergymen of any other faith. Opposition to American involvement in the Korean conflict was strongest within the Protestant clergy. Also strongest is Protestant opposition to the manufacture and testing of atomic and nuclear weapons.

Protestantism is also most vigorous in its defense of the rights of individual pacifists or conscientious objectors. A number of Protestant denominations (e.g., Friends, Brethren, Mennonites) are pacifist as a matter of church doctrine and discipline; all recognize the right of individual conscientious objection. Three centuries ago the Puritan Army Council presented to Parliament a proposed bill of rights, one provision of which stated that "the matter of impressing and constraining any of us to serve in the wars is against our freedom." This proposal was not accepted by Parliament, just as Madison's proposal a century and a half later to add to the American Bill of Rights a proviso that "no person religiously scrupulous shall be compelled to bear arms" was not accepted by Congress. Protestantism's defense of the right of individual conscience in the matter of bearing arms is thus understandable as a long tradition. It is also understandable in the light of the general sanctity of individual conscience in the Protestant ethic.

Undoubtedly the pro-pacificism of Protestantism is in large degree shared by American Judaism. Judaism too has a long tradition of pacificism. In the post-World War I period rabbis and rabbinic organizations, particularly of the Reform wing, joined in the many peace organizations and movements. The fact, however, that Jews were the chief victims of Nazism undoubtedly had a profound effect in altering the general pro-pacifist attitude of American Judaism. It is a fair guess that even before Pearl Harbor most rabbis in the United States deemed American entry into the war necessary, unavoidable, and completely justified.

Today Judaism is again close to Protestantism in seeking the total abolition of war. During the period of the "cold war," when pro-pacificism was equated in many nationalist and Catholic organizations with pro-communism or at best insensibility to the Communist menace, the voice of the rabbi was mostly stilled. Only a relatively few rabbis signed the Stockholm peace petition (although in all probability the majority agreed with its purpose). A large number, but perhaps still no more than a minority, later called for the cessation of the manufacture and testing of nuclear weapons. Of course, as the need to prevent a nuclear war becomes increasingly recognized, it is to be expected that the pro-pacificism of American Judaism will become more articulate.

American Catholicism has no sympathy with conscientious objection. This is not surprising. Catholic philosophy is hardly hospitable to the concept of individual conscience. Catholic principles require the faithful to respect and obey duly constituted authority provided that faith and morals are not endangered, and it is the Church and not the individual that determines whether particular state action endangers faith and morals.

Surprising, however, is the intensity of American Catholicism's opposition to general pacificism. Among the religious groups Catholicism has been most vigorous in its defense of America's involvement in the Korean conflict, its use of the atom bomb, its maintenance of a strong military establishment and its taking a hard line in negotiating peace with the Soviets. While there is no discernible single Catholic position on the United Nations, Catholicism evinces considerably less enthusiasm for that organization than does Protestantism, and certainly less than Judaism. Along with the veterans groups, Catholic publications often equate pro-pacificism with pro-communism and condemn demands for cessation of the manufacture or testing of nuclear weapons as playing into the hands of the Communists.

What is slightly puzzling about this is the fact that here too American Catholicism appears to be more Catholic than the Pope. Not only was the Vatican neutral all during World War II, but it early and often expressed belief in the need to eliminate war and to bring an end to the dreadful race in atomic armaments. With all its opposition to communism, the Vatican seems a good deal more hospitable to the idea of peaceful coexistence than does American Catholicism.

Once again the explanation lies at least partly in terms of cultural competition. The same motivation—adjustment to the nationalist values in American culture—that helps to explain the intensity of the anti-communism of American Catholics helps to explain the intensity of their anti-pacificism.

SOVIET COMMUNISM AND THE IRON CURTAIN

American Catholicism is not only more intense in its opposition to domestic communism than either of the other two major faiths, but also uncompromising in its enmity to Soviet or international communism. It considers the East-West struggle a war between Christianity and atheism, between God and the Antichrist, an Armageddon in which obviously there can be no compromise.

Here, too, the intensity of its anti-communism occasionally proves embarrassing. Its anti-Sovietism includes not only Soviet Russia but all the countries of the Soviet bloc. Its condemnation of Soviet Russia is matched by its condemnation of Poland, Hungary, and other east European countries controlled by Communists. The news, therefore, that the Polish hierarchy, with the approval of the Vatican, had arrived at a *modus vivendi* with the Communist government of Poland imposed upon the Catholic Church in America the task of explanation and justification. This was not easy since the Catholic press had until then taken the consistent position that the Communist governments were so completely evil and so devoid of honor that any attempt of settlement with them would be both immoral and ineffectual. Nor was the task made any easier by the fact that as part of the settlement the atheistic Polish Communist government agreed to reintroduce religious instruction in the public schools.

What was particularly embarrassing about this concession was that the principal or one of the principal counts in American Catholicism's indictment of the east European and Asian Communist governments was and continues to be their restrictions upon religious liberty and freedom of worship. There has been a host of books, articles, and lectures on religion behind the iron curtain, produced in America under Catholic sponsorship reflecting the views of the Catholic Church and all painting the picture in the darkest colors. Cardinal Mindszenty, Archbishop Stepinac, and other Roman Catholic priests and prelates imprisoned behind the iron curtain are all considered martyrs to the cause of religious freedom. Provisions in the constitution of Soviet Russia and the other Russian satellite countries purporting to assure freedom of worship as well as protestations from official governmental sources are completely discounted. Great weight is placed upon reports by emigrees from east Europe and Catholic missionaries coming out of Communist China, and information originating from underground sources, all of which belie the constitutional provisions and official statements, and indicate a reign of terror not only against the Roman Catholic Church but also against all churches and religions. How, Catholics ask with a logic difficult to meet, can one expect freedom of religion from a political system that deems religion an enemy of the people and is committed to its extirpation?

Catholics are particularly bitter about the relative Protestant silence on the persecution of Roman Catholics behind the iron curtain. They contrast this with the Protestants' vociferous protestations against alleged persecution of Protestants in Spain, in Colombia, and in other Catholic-influenced countries. They ask whether the Protestants are not applying a double standard and whether religious persecution and infringements upon freedom of worship are less horrendous when committed by non-Catholic states than when committed by Catholic states.

It is indisputable that Protestantism is a good deal less pessimistic than Catholicism about the status of religion behind the iron curtain. Protestant clergymen who visit Soviet Russia return with reports that are considerably more charitable to the Communists in respect to their treatment of religion than can be found in any Catholic publications. They are more likely than are the Catholics to give credence to the declarations of churchmen inside Soviet Russia that they do enjoy freedom of worship and are not subject to persecution by the government.

Protestants can hardly be under any illusions as to the Communist view of religion and the ultimate Communist goal in respect to religion. Nor can they be unaware of the violent anti-religious activities of the revolutionary Soviet government or of the Communist governments in the satellite countries upon their coming to power. They find, however, some measure of justification for this in the reactionary policies and practices of the Orthodox Church in Russia during the Czarist era and of the Roman Catholic Church in east Europe in the period between the wars. They do not look at Mindszenty, Stepinac, and the other Roman Catholic prelates as religious martyrs but as political activists. They are inclined to believe that Russia's obvious desire to reach a rapprochement with the West will cause it to subordinate its long-term goal of eliminating religion and for an indefinite period will ameliorate the condition of the churches and of religion behind the iron curtain.

In its attitude toward religion behind the iron curtain, American Judaism is closer to Catholicism than to Protestantism—one of the rare instances when this is so. Rabbis who have visited Soviet Russia are as pessimistic about the future of Judaism in that country as are Catholics about the future of Christianity. They give as little credence as the Catholics to the assertions of the few remaining rabbis in Russia that they enjoy full freedom of worship and religious liberty.

The Jewish religious organizations, however, are more subdued than the Catholics in their condemnation of Soviet Russia on this score. The reason is that they see little to be gained by this tactic. Resigned to the view that there is no future for Judaism in Russia, they prefer to concentrate their energies in efforts to persuade the Soviet government to permit free emigration so that the remnant of Jewry that still so wishes may start a new life in Israel, the United States, or some other country where the political climate is more hospitable to religion in general and Judaism in particular.

AMBASSADOR TO THE VATICAN

Although dormant at the time of this writing, the question of an exchange of ambassadors between the United States and the Vatican remains a potential source of serious Protestant-Catholic controversy. With the exception of the inclusion of parochial schools in a program for Federal aid to education, no secular issue so unites American Protestantism as does that of diplomatic recognition of the Holy See. Nothing has a more potent catalytic effect in arousing political action by Protestantism. When in 1950 President Truman announced his intention of sending General Mark W. Clark to the Vatican as an ambassador, Protestantism showed clearly that it had not forgotten the skills it had acquired in its earlier political crusades and that it could still match the Catholic Church in mobilizing effective political action when it believed the stakes sufficiently high. Protestant ministers throughout the nation preached sermons against the proposal. The National Council of Churches joined forces with Protestants and Other Americans United for Separation of Church and State in meeting the threat. During the course of the controversy the White House was flooded with mail on the issue. A White House count indicated that the communications ran six to one against the proposal, thus effectively burying it, at least for the time being.

Protestants see in American recognition of the Holy See a flagrant violation of the principle of separation of church and state. Even those Protestants who view the First Amendment to the Federal Constitution in the narrow sense as not barring all government intervention in religious matters but merely as prohibiting preferential treatment of a particular faith regard the sending of an ambassador to the Vatican as a violation of the principle of separation of church and state on the ground that it would constitute preferential treatment of the Catholic Church. (The explanation for the Protestant view that an exchange of ambassadors and diplomatic recognition of the Vatican would be conferring benefit upon it may be principally psychological. Certainly the point is not legally analogous to grant-ing tax-raised funds to parochial schools.)

Catholic churchmen find it difficult to understand the intensity of Protestant feeling on this issue. They consider an exchange of ambassadors with the Vatican as merely normal action in interna-tional affairs. They point out that the overwhelming majority of other nations, including some in which church and state are sepa-rated and others in which Protestantism is the established religion, maintain diplomatic relations with the Vatican. They argue that aside from being the head of the Catholic Church, the Pope is also the ruler of a geographically small but nevertheless recognized inde-pendent state. They see no difference between recognition of the Vatican and recognition of Israel. Finally, they suggest that Protes-tant opposition to diplomatic recognition indirectly helps the cause of communism, since the United States and the Vatican are the two major opponents of international communism, and refusal to allow them to pool their efforts through normal diplomatic channels ren-ders each less effective in meeting the threat.

Nevertheless, Catholic churchmen recognize the depth of Protes-tant feeling and have studiously refrained from making an all-out effort to secure an ambassador to the Holy See. While they of course strongly favor the step, they do not have anything like the sense of injustice about it that they have about the exclusion of parochial schools from programs of aid to education out of tax-raised funds. They do not consider the matter of major importance nor its effec-tuation worth the interreligious acrimony that it has engendered.

Jewish religious bodies have maintained a discreet silence on the issue, although there have been occasional public statements by indi-vidual rabbis. Generally, it may be said that with rare exceptions the American rabbinate is opposed in principle to an exchange of am-bassadors with the Vatican.

ISRAEL, ZIONISM, AND THE ARABS

The establishment of the state of Israel and the subsequent prob-lem of American-Israeli relations have undoubtedly proved a source of interreligious difficulties. During the period of Israel's invasion of the Sinai Peninsula the problem of Arab-Israel relations imposed a severe strain on the *entent cordiale* between American Protestantism

and American Judaism. So long as the problem of Arab-Israel relations remains unsolved it will continue to be a potentially serious
source of Jewish-Christian disharmony in the United States.

It is hardly disputable that the overwhelming majority of American rabbis are sympathetic to Zionist aspirations and identify themselves with the welfare of Israel. Few indeed are the rabbis in
America who have not already either made at least one trip to Israel
or made plans for a trip—trips undertaken in much the same spirit
as a pilgrimage. Twenty-five years ago there was not nearly such
unanimity of sympathy for Zionist aspirations among the American
rabbinate. The advent of Hitler and the consequent mass extermination of European Jewry has convinced all but an insignificant hand-
ful of rabbis in the United States that the security of Israel must be
preserved if for no other reason than to provide a place of refuge
should virulent anti-Semitism again rise. Moreover, they see no other
place for those Jews who can come out from behind the iron curtain, particularly in view of America's stringent anti-immigration
policy. Besides these factors, most rabbis and Jewish organizations
are convinced that the interests of democratic America would best
be served by protecting the young democracy in the Middle East.
Finally, American rabbis would be less than human (or more, de-
pending upon how one looks at it) if they did not feel some sense
of prideful identification with the little new nation that managed
to establish and maintain itself against what appeared to be such
overwhelming odds.

American rabbis and religious organizations are hardly insensitive
to the charge of dual loyalty leveled against them by the bitterly
anti-Zionist American Council for Judaism—an organization as alien
to the mainstream of Jewish opinion as was Rabbi Benjamin Shultz'
American Jewish League Against Communism. Surprisingly enough,
similar charges are leveled only occasionally from Christian sources.
Zionists meet these charges by pointing to American Catholicism's
sympathy for Ireland in its long struggle for independence from
Britain. This sympathy, they urge, did not in any degree prejudice
Catholic loyalty to the United States, and there is therefore no reason for supposing that American Jewry's sympathy for Israel in its
struggle for independence and survival will prejudice Jewish loyalty
to the United States.

There is no discernible unified position within Protestantism on
Israel or Zionism. On the one extreme is the strongly anti-Zionist

Christian Century whose anti-Israel editorial policy has, however, mellowed considerably in recent years, indicating a recognition that Israel is here to stay and that it would be wiser for the Arab states to recognize that fact. On the other extreme are the pro-Zionist *Churchman* and the Protestant ministers affiliated with the American Christian Palestine Committee.

The majority of Protestant clergymen stand somewhere in between. It is probable, though not empirically verified, that they are sympathetic to Israel and to Zionist aspirations. Their pro-democrat feelings would naturally incline them sympathetically to a small democratic state surrounded by a host of non-democratic and politically backward Arab nations. In addition, the close working relations between them and American rabbis and Jewish organizations in so many common causes could be expected to incline them favorably toward a conviction held so earnestly by their Jewish friends. Finally, they too recognize that virulent anti-Semitism cannot be wholly relegated to the past and that there may again be need for a place of refuge.

But this last consideration also brings Protestant clergymen into disagreement with Judaism. For they express a similar concern with the Arab refugees and assert that it is wrong to make refugees out of Arabs in order to find a home for Jewish refugees. While many of them concede that the return of all or most of the Arab refugees to their original homes in what is now the state of Israel is unrealistic and impracticable, they remain troubled and will probably restrain their instinctive sympathy for Israel and Zionism until the problem of the Arab refugees is satisfactorily settled. Another cause of friction is the Protestants' antipathy toward nationalism and the suspicion that some of them still harbor regarding Israel's future intentions. The Israel invasion of Egypt appeared at the time to lend support to the fears that imperialistic ambitions were not absent in Israel, although events since that time, particularly the pro-Sovietism of Nasser's Egypt, have largely eased these fears.

The Catholic Church in America is on the whole neutral on the question of Israel. Again empirical verification is impossible, but it is probable that the neutrality veers to the unfriendly, and this notwithstanding the cordial relations between Soviet Russia and the United Arab Republic of Egypt and Syria. The Church is, however, particularly and deeply concerned with one aspect of the Israel problem—the internationalization of Jerusalem. It believes that the birthplace of Christianity and the site of so many of its historic religious shrines should not be under the control of either the Jews or the Arabs, but should be governed by an international agency. The internationalization of Jerusalem is likely to remain for some time the principal focus of Catholic interest in Israel.

9. THE CONSEQUENCES OF COMPETITION

THE THESIS RESTATED

It is convenient at this point briefly to restate the thesis of this book.

Religious groups (and presumably, non-religious as well), avowedly or not, seek to translate their own particular hierarchy of social values into categorical imperatives for the community at large, including those members of the community outside their own respective folds. Each religious group, consciously or unconsciously, attempts to shape the culture of the community according to its own concept of the good life. Since government and law are a highly potent and effective means of translating particular values into universal rules of conduct, each competing religious group will seek to prevail upon the government to accept its particular values as the best. In a democracy it is presumed that the government will generally act in accordance with the wishes of the people. Hence, cultural competition among religious groups will center mainly on public issues, with each of the various religious groups endeavoring to convince the people that its particular position on a specific public issue is most desirable and the most just.

Since in a multi-religious (and non-religious) nation such as the United States no single religious group is likely to have sufficient adherents, both within and without its formal membership, to fashion the culture of the community according to its own values, the result will be a series of alliances in specific areas among groups whose values are most closely akin in each of the areas. For a century and a half America's political culture—i.e., its concepts of the nature of the state and its proper relation to the individual, of civil rights and

153.

liberties, and particularly of the relationship of church and state—has been fashioned by an alliance of Protestant dissent and secular humanism. Its moral culture, on the other hand, particularly as concretized in its penal codes, has been fashioned by an alliance of Protestant dissent and Calvinist Puritanism.

During the past quarter century a new and increasingly more powerful competitor has risen to challenge this dual monopoly. In many respects the moral concepts of this new competitor—Roman Catholicism—are closely akin to those of Calvinist Puritanism, both being predicated in large measure on the premise that mortification of the flesh is a good. Hence, in matters of morality, Roman Catholicism (except where overriding economic considerations are present, as in the case of bingo) has quite eagerly joined the alliance of Calvinism and Protestant dissent. Indeed, because the alliance between Protestant dissent (into which New England Calvinism merged after the disestablishment of the New England Congregational churches during the first third of the nineteenth century) and secular humanism has recently been having significant liberalizing effects upon Protestant moral values, Roman Catholicism is rapidly becoming the chief protagonist and defender of Calvinist Puritanism.

In political culture, however, Roman Catholicism has no ideological kinship to the alliance of secular humanism and Protestant dissent. It has challenged many of the assumptions of this alliance and has offered to the American people a number of assumptions at variance with those of the Protestant-humanist alliance. For example, its concept of the desirability of a close and co-operative relation between religion and the state is diametrically opposed to the concept of complete separation espoused by Protestant dissent and secular humanism.

Even more recently another competitor, Judaism, has entered the market place. Ideologically it is or has become most closely akin to secular humanism. While its numbers are too small and are not likely in the near future to become large enough for it to be a serious contender by itself, the weight it adds to the Protestant dissent-secular humanist alliance is by no means inconsiderable, and in a particular case may prove decisive. Religion in the public schools may be such a case. It is quite possible that secular humanism and those elements within Protestantism that are committed to a completely secular public school could not alone ward off the efforts of the Catholic-Protestant alliance aimed at bringing religion into the schools, but that the added weight of a united Jewry may be sufficient to swing the balance.

Generally it may be suggested that on the overwhelming majority of public issues in which the competitors are divided, secular humanism and Judaism will be found on the one side and Roman Catholicism on the opposite. Protestantism is usually to be found in the middle, sometimes veering toward the one alliance, sometimes toward the other. However, more and more the trend of Protestantism appears to be toward the humanist-Jewish alliance, so that it can be said that with some notable exceptions Protestantism will generally be found on the same side with humanism and Judaism, and opposed to Catholicism on matters of public importance in which there is division among the competing forces.

COMPETITION AND CONFLICT

With this restatement of the thesis of this book, we can consider some of the consequences of competition in the market of religious cultures. The most obvious consequence (concomitant might perhaps be more accurate) of competition is conflict. No observer of the contemporary scene can fail to note the interreligious tension, acrimony, and disharmony that almost inevitably accompanies divisions among the faiths on public issues. To get a fair idea of this, one need only observe the slings and arrows that Protestants and Other Americans United for Separation of Church and State and Catholic churchmen and publications cast at one another. Or one can read the Protestant and Catholic press when a bill is presented in the legislature to include parochial schools in a program of free bus transportation, or during an incident such as the Hildy adoption affair.

It is generally accepted that conflict among religious groups is to be deplored; that it is an evil or a misfortune which should be prevented at all costs. The National Conference of Christians and Jews was established on that premise and its mission remains to foster harmony and eliminate conflict among Protestants, Catholics, and Jews.

Even if it be accepted that conflict among religious groups is in all cases unfortunate and undesirable, the twofold question remains whether it can practicably be avoided and if so whether the consequences of avoidance may not be even more unfortunate and undesirable than the conflict itself. Where differences are deep-seated and sincerely held it would be fatuous to expect that conflict can be avoided by seeking to submerge the differences and pretending they do not exist. That is the major approach of the National Conference of Christians and Jews, which as a matter of policy will not enter into "controversial" issues—i.e., those in which Protestants, Catholics, and Jews differ. And that, I suggest, is the principal reason for the singular lack of success on the part of the National Conference in coping with the problems of tensions and conflicts among the religious faiths. Instead of meeting the problems it avoids them.

Another method of seeking to prevent interreligious conflict, a method still highly popular and sometimes called "intercultural education," is by fostering "understanding." This is the principal method of the National Conference of Christians and Jews. It is based on the assumption that since religious persons are necessarily good persons the conflict among them can only be explained by lack of understanding. If each faith were sufficiently familiar with the beliefs, practices, and ideals of the other faiths, misunderstanding would disappear and along with it conflict, and both would be superseded by understanding, sympathy, and harmony.

One difficulty with this approach is that the very act of bringing knowledge and understanding may itself be a contributor to conflict and disharmony. Catholic doctrine forbids the faithful as a general rule to study and learn the practices and beliefs of other faiths. Indeed, the Canon Law declares it to be a grave sin for a Catholic knowingly to read a non-Catholic version of the Bible. For that reason, as I understand it, the National Conference does not issue general reading lists, but restricts itself to separate Protestant, Catholic, and Jewish reading lists. Of course, it is immediately obvious that this is self-defeating; for if the members of each faith read only the books on their own lists they will not get the knowledge and understanding of the other faiths which is presumed to be the best means of eliminating or ameliorating interfaith conflict.

Moreover, if the three faiths are explained in one book (as in the book by Florence Mary Fitch, *One God—The Ways We Worship Him*), it would hardly improve interfaith relations to give one faith more prominence or more favorable treatment than the others or to state expressly that the faiths were not equal in merit or validity but that only one (named) faith has true merit and validity. Yet it is directly contrary to Catholic doctrine to present the various faiths in such a way as to give rise to the impression that they are equal in merit and validity. It is exactly for this reason that, on objections by the Catholic Church, the Fitch book was removed from the approved reading list of the New York public schools.

A far more serious difficulty with the approach of ameliorating interfaith conflict through understanding is the questionable validity of the basic premise. The assumption that out of knowledge and understanding come sympathy and harmony has, as far as I know, never been empirically established. On the contrary, among the most extreme enemies of each of the three faiths have been converts who at one time were members, and often clerics, of the particular faith and thus had a knowledge and understanding of the practices, beliefs, and ideals of the faith they discarded superior to that which could be expected of even well-informed members of another faith. I venture to suggest that the most vigorous critics of other faiths today have a much higher than average knowledge of the practices, beliefs, and ideals of the faiths they criticize and oppose. I doubt that Paul Blanshard's intensive study of Roman Catholicism has made him friendlier to or more sympathetic with it than before he started.

Another method employed to eliminate interreligious conflict is to find a common enemy upon which all the faiths can vent their aggressive urges. This too has been essayed—though naturally not avowed—by the National Conference of Christians and Jews. It has sought to associate the three faiths in common efforts against secularism and against communism. The crusade against secularism has caused the Conference at times to flirt with the idea of bringing religion into the public schools, and this has of course not enhanced its popularity with the Jewish community. While the crusade against communism has not alienated anybody, I very much doubt that it has had much effect in ameliorating interfaith conflict.

A final method for reducing interfaith conflict is compromise. If the Catholics want a lot of religion in the public schools and the Jews want none, let us compromise by having a little religion in the schools—perhaps a released-time program, or perhaps a program for teaching moral and spiritual values. If the Catholics want full public support for their schools and the Protestants demand that they shall not have a penny, let us restore interfaith harmony through a sensible compromise. Let the Protestants give a little, and let the Catholics give a little. Let us go half way, as for example by paying for bus transportation of children but not for the salaries of teachers.

Again I express doubt as to the efficacy of the solution. If—and that is the assumption of this book—differences among the religious faiths are founded upon basic differences of ideology and principle and the good-way-of-life, I question whether we have the moral right to ask compromise even to avoid interfaith conflict. And even if compromise is forthcoming, it is by no means certain that harmony will follow. In an all-out contest ending with one contestant victorious and the other defeated, at least one party is happy. In a compromise as often as not both parties are unhappy and discontented. Finally, compromise too often merely postpones but does not prevent conflict. The Catholic Church, for example, has been frank to assert that it regards bus transportation as no more than a temporary compromise and that its ultimate objective still is to obtain a full partnership for parochial schools in the nation's educational system.

I suggest that there is no practicable way to eliminate conflict save by eliminating competition. Conflict is the price that must be paid for competition and there is no way of obtaining competition unless we are willing to pay the price. This is true not only of competition in religious cultures but of all competition—competition in tangible wares, in political objectives, in artistic convictions, in economic theories. Baseball teams will on occasions break into fistfights in the heat of a game. Republicans, Democrats, Socialists, and Communists will often defame one another. Members of the Senate and of the House of Representatives have been known to exchange blows in the chambers of the Capitol. The relations between those who loved Senator McCarthy and those who despised him were hardly less acrimonious than the relations among Protestants, Catholics, and Jews. When opposing beliefs on the most important things in life are deeply held, only those who are not lower than the angels can be expected to be able always to avoid conflict.

THE USES OF CONFLICT

This should hardly be surprising to a civilization whose religion and morality are based upon Christian theological concepts. For Christianity presupposes a state of perennial conflict between good and evil until the ultimate conflict at Armageddon and the Second Coming of the Messiah. If religions held by others are not evil, they are certainly not quite as good as the true Christian faith (whether, in the particular case that be Catholicism, a denomination of Protestantism, or any of the Eastern churches). If that were not so, there would be no moral justification for the missionary mandate in the most missionary of all faiths.

The truth of the matter is that conflict is the indispensable ingredient of progress in any field, religious, social, political, economic, etc. In an article in the 1956 issue of *The Journal of Social Issues*, Don J. Hager has acutely pointed out the uses of conflict in a democratic society. "Social science," he states, "seems to have forgotten that conflict is a form of social interaction. It relieves tensions. It forces the contending groups to modify their claims. It is often the only way that groups may express opposition to ideas and practices they abhor. Uncontrolled conflict (and violence) can be destructive, but the important task of creating and maintaining a productive social system is subverted by denying the efficacy of conflict in stabilizing the social order and advancing the commonweal."

Every advance in religion—or what its adherents consider an advance—came as result of conflict between the old and the better new. When Elijah stood at Mount Carmel and taunted the priests of Baal he certainly was not practicing good interfaith relations. When Jesus inveighed against the hypocrisies of the Pharisees his conduct was not such as would have been approved by a contemporary Imperial Conference of Christians and Jews. When Luther chose the Eve of All Saints' to post his Ninety-five Theses on the door of the church at Wittenberg he was hardly contributing to religious peace and harmony. So long as humanity is less than perfect and so long as room remains for advance in our social, religious, political, economic, artistic, and intellectual civilizations, and so long as man is blessed or cursed with that divine spark which impels advance, conflict will always be with us.

Again to quote Dr. Hager, "The important task is not, therefore, the indiscriminate and undisciplined elimination of conflict but, rather, the creation and preservation of devices whereby conflict can be made socially productive." In the terms of this book and its thesis, conflict is competition, and the important thing is to evolve and adhere to rules of fair competition to insure that the greatest possible social productivity emerges from the competition between religious cultures.

RULES OF FAIR COMPETITION

The rules of fair competition most likely to achieve the desired end come naturally and logically out of the nature of the American experiment. That experiment, as I have suggested in the first chapter, assumes that in a free market of ideas and ideologies the American people can be counted upon in the long run to choose what is best, that the best test of truth is its acceptance in the free market of ideas, that given light the people will choose the right way. From this it follows that fair competition means such competition as most nearly allows Americans to make a free and informed choice, and such competition is unfair (and self-defeating) as interferes with, or restricts the exercise of, a free and informed choice. On this basis, I suggest the following as a few of the elementary rules of fair competition.

1. The use of force must at all times be condemned and rejected. God is not necessarily on the side with the heaviest artillery nor truth on the side with the largest armies. The superiority of Christianity over Islam was not established by the fact that the Crusaders had more effective means of destroying life than had the Saracens, nor its superiority over Judaism established by the fact that the Jews found along the route were too few and too weak to resist their slaughter by the Holy Crusaders. On the contrary, as has often been pointed out, resort to force is an admission of the moral and intellectual weakness of one's claims. The great success of the American experiment lies in the fact that we have eliminated the use of force in resolving religious conflicts.

2. The suppression of any sect or of its activities must at all times be condemned and rejected. This rule is really a particular application of the previous one. Unfortunately it cannot be said that America has always abided by it. Jehovah's Witnesses were, and to some extent remain, the victims of community efforts at suppression. The abortive attempt of the State of New York to suppress the motion picture *The Miracle* because the Catholic Church deemed it sacrilegious is another illustration of the use of suppression in competition among religious cultures—as indeed is the entire concept of govern-

mentally prohibited sacrilege or blasphemy. The suppression of ideas or arguments is directly opposed to the concept of free and fair competition.

3. The involvement of government must at all times be avoided. Even if the government does not employ its coercive powers, its intervention in favor of some religion or of all religions prejudices free choice by the people. Social scientists have long recognized that laws have an educational no less than a coercive effect, and that the people generally will recognize and adhere to standards and values publicly espoused by their government. It is for that reason that state manifestations of religiosity are to be avoided if we are to have free competition among religious cultures.

4. Use of ecclesiastical sanctions to affect governmental activity must be avoided. This is a corollary of the previous rule. If the government is to avoid use of secular sanctions to further religious policy, the church must not use ecclesiastical sanctions to coerce or influence governmental action. It is entirely proper and appropriate for the Catholic Church to preach the evils of divorce and to appeal to its communicants and to the people at large to elect as their representatives those who recognize the evils of divorce and are pledged to eliminate them by restricting or prohibiting divorce. It is an entirely different matter for the Church to forbid state judges who are of the Catholic faith to deny divorces to litigants, Catholic or non-Catholic, who are entitled to them by the laws of the state, or to command them to act any way differently in a divorce case than in a case arising out of an automobile accident or the non-payment of a promissory note.

5. Verbal blows should be avoided. Just as physical force prejudices free informed choice so do verbal blows or verbal acts. The term "verbal act" was used by the United States Supreme Court to describe the type of expression not protected by the freedom of speech guaranty of the Constitution. In upholding the conviction of a Jehovah's Witness who was accused of having said to a police official, "You are a God damned racketeer, and a damned Fascist," the Court said: "There are certain well-defined and narrowly limited classes of speech, the prevention and punishment of which has never been thought to raise any Constitutional problem. These include the lewd and obscene, the profane, the libelous, and the insulting or 'fighting' words—those which by their very utterance inflict injury or tend to incite an immediate breach of the peace. It has well been

observed that such utterances are no essential part of any exposition of ideas and are of such slight social value as a step to truth that any benefit that may be derived from them is clearly outweighed by the social interest in order and morality."

Within the terms of our discussion verbal blows consist of appeals exclusively to passions and prejudices. The complete avoidence of emotionalism in discussions of principles deeply held is neither possible nor desirable. It is, however, both possible and desirable to avoid irrelevancies which impassion rather than convince. Personal attacks on individuals, whether they be Cardinal Spellman or Bishop Oxnam, have little relevancy to the merits of their respective positions on public issues and impair rather than promote a free, enlightened choice by the people.

Within the same category I would put deliberate or careless misrepresentation of motive. As examples I would cite the frequent charge that the sole or principal objective of the Catholic Church in America is the attainment of power and the exercise of power for its own sake. As I have previously indicated, I believe this to be untrue and unfair. I can see no logical or moral difference between the desire of Catholicism to "catholicize" America, i.e., convert it to Catholic philosophy, religion, and way of living, and the desire of Protestantism or secular humanism to convert or keep America loyal to their philosophies, religions, and way of living. Nor do I see in the one any more evidence of a struggle for power for its own sake than the others.

Also in this category I would put the equally frequent charge that those opposing the Catholic position on such issues as extension of bus transportation to parochial school children are motivated by anti-Catholic bigotry and prejudice. I do not think that Cardinal Spellman either helped the Catholic cause or advanced freedom of enlightened choice when he charged Mrs. Eleanor Roosevelt with bigotry for opposing Federal aid to parochial schools. The same can be said of the action of the Connecticut hierarchy which in 1957 accused of bigotry those legislators who opposed a bill to extend free bus transportation to parochial schools. Finally, in this category too I would put charges of pro-atheism or pro-communism levelled against those who oppose what they deem violations of the principle of separation of church and state.

6. Chauvinism should be avoided. This rule is related to the preceding one. An argument that a certain position on a public issue is

bad because it is not American while the contrary position is good because it is American is in the nature of an appeal to prejudice and hinders rather than aids free, enlightened choice. It is one thing to argue that separation of church and state has been tried in America for a century and three quarters and has worked well, whereas union of church and state was tried in the old world and worked ill. It is something else to say that separation of church and state is American and therefore good while union of church and state is un-American and therefore bad. This appeal to nationalism and ancestor worship is particularly inappropriate in a nation whose entire population (except for a few surviving Redmen) is alien and whose culture and traditions are largely imported. Secular humanism, it should be remembered, is a direct descendant of French Enlightenment and deism. Of all the competitors in the cultural arena, Catholicism has been the principal victim of chauvinism in cultural competition. Fair competition requires that every proposal be adjudged on its own merits.

7. Economic boycotts should be avoided. I do not refer to the urgings of clergymen to their communicants not to purchase salacious literature, or even to the imposition of ecclesiastical sanctions to that end. That is entirely an internal matter of church doctrine and discipline. What I refer to is economic boycott designed to influence the actions of non-communicants, e.g., boycotting a theater and all its films for exhibiting one objectionable film, or a bookstore for selling one or several objectionable books. This is unfair competition because it prejudices free enlightened choice by the use of economic force to restrict expression.

THE CHURCH IN POLITICS

Conflict has been the first clear consequence of cultural competition. The second has been the intensive participation of church groups in political activity. One who follows the workings of the courts and legislatures or indeed reads the daily press cannot fail to notice how often representatives of religious groups appear before legislative committees to urge enactment or defeat of a particular measure, or present briefs as "friend of the court" in litigation involving social issues.

It should not be assumed that this active interest on the part of church groups is a recent phenomenon. As has been pointed out earlier, the church has been in American politics since the conflict between the Patriots and the Loyalists at the time of the Revolutionary War. The abolition of slavery, prohibition of intoxicating liquors, and anti-obscenity laws are all concrete results of the (Protestant) church in politics.

In the light of this background it ill becomes Protestants to condemn and criticize the political activity of the Catholic Church. Certain types of political activity on the part of the Catholic Church I believe to be wrong. It is wrong to impose ecclesiastical sanctions to influence the actions of governmental officials. It is wrong for the Church to enter politics as a party or to sponsor and support a political party, such as a Christian Democrat Party or a Catholic Center Party. It is also wrong for the Church to have *de facto* representatives in the government. This practice, unfortunately, is happening with increasing frequency. There is a tendency to divide political offices and appointive positions among the religious faiths according to some kind of quota. (In New York City, for example, the nine members of the board of education are divided among the three major faiths; probation officers in the children's court are appointed in accordance with a religious quota corresponding to the distribution among the three faiths of children appearing in the court; both major parties make sure that in the city and in the state elections each of the three faiths is represented on the top level of the election ballot, etc.). The result is that a person, if not nominated by the Catholic Church, is often at least subject to Church veto. In consequence, the nominee or appointee will feel that he owes his position to the Church or that he will be required to remain in its good graces to retain his position. He is therefore likely to conduct himself in his office as a *de facto* representative of the Church.

I do not, however, think it improper or undesirable for the Church to take political action in order to procure the election of candidates who support its views or the defeat of those who oppose them. I think it was entirely proper for the Catholic bishops in Connecticut to warn legislators that how they vote on the parochial school bus bill would be remembered on Election Day. It would, of course, have been equally proper for Protestant ministers to issue the same warning. It has long been the policy of labor unions to reward their friends and punish their enemies on Election Day.

Negro groups are not criticized for urging the election of candidates sympathetic to Negro claims and the defeat of those opposed to Negro claims. Today the complexities of social life have made inevitable group participation as well as individual participation in political action.

COMPETITION AND CHANGE

The most important consequence of cultural competition is change, change both within and without the competing groups. Within the competing groups there have been, as we have seen, numerous changes in positions on public issues. Some have been merely changes dictated by strategy. For example, Catholic philosophy and doctrine have always been unfriendly to a public educational system devoid of religious teachings and practices. When Catholicism in America was an insular, weak, and unprotected minority it strongly opposed religious teachings and practices in the public school because they were and inevitably would be Protestant teachings and practices. When, however, Catholicism became strong and felt it could hold its own in the competition it reverted to its natural position of hostility to secular education.

Similarly, the Catholic opposition to anti-lottery and anti-gambling laws after flirting with the idea of supporting them was dictated by the strategic need to find new sources of revenue for financing the vast self-supported Catholic educational system. Other strategic changes on the part of Catholicism include its willingness to compromise on indirect or auxiliary benefits to parochial school children in lieu of incorporating such schools as full partners in public educational financing, its reconciliation to the public school system (which, at the beginning, it bitterly opposed), and its willingness to allow Catholic children to participate in "non-sectarian" prayer and teachings in the public schools.

There is, I submit, nothing invidious in these strategic changes of positions. So long as they are not misrepresented as being something that they are not, there is no just cause for complaint. If Catholicism believes that parochial schools are morally entitled to share in tax-raised funds as equal partners, it has every right to press for half-way measures that appear to be attainable. If the Catholic Church believes that the best society is one in which all the members are faithful

Catholics and in which church and state are united to promote the cause of God and Christ, it has every right, and indeed a solemn duty, to seek to achieve that end in America and in the interim (which, Catholicism concedes, may be of indefinite duration) to accept the half-way measure of equal governmental aid for all churches.

Strategic changes of position have not been absent from Protestantism. Its acceptance of a secular public school system was dictated by the strategic necessity of meeting Catholicism's just claim to share in public funds along with Protestant public schools. The establishment of the National Council of Churches and Protestantism's ecumenical drive are, I believe, in no small measure strategic counteractions to the rising tide of Catholicism. So too is the entry of Protestantism in the field of political activity on an organized day-to-day basis instead of sporadic political crusades such as those against slavery, obscenity, and the evil of liquor.

More significant than strategic changes of positions on public issues have been the changes in ideologies, principles, and ways of life effected by cultural competition. Most prominent have been those experienced by Protestantism, resulting in large measure from its alliance with secular humanism. Consider what has happened to the two established churches in America, the Congregational Church in New England and the Anglican (Protestant Episcopal) Church in the South. Today these two churches are among the most stalwart champions of the principle of separation of church and state. (The small fragment within Episcopalianism that even refuses to use the word "Protestant" in its name is hardly of much significance.) The major Protestant publication in America most closely reflecting the secular-humanist point of view is the Protestant Episcopal *Churchman*. It is perhaps but a slight exaggeration to say that its alliance with secular humanism has made of other-world Protestantism a this-world religion.

Judaism too has experienced much change in outlook and way of life as a consequence of cultural competition. Of all the groups it has adjusted itself most completely and most happily to the values of secular humanism. When one compares the Judaism of mid-twentieth-century America with the Judaism of mid-nineteenth-century eastern Europe, one can see the radical changes effected by this alliance.

Of the three major faiths cultural competition has had the least effect upon Roman Catholicism in ideology, principles, and way of life. This is understandable for a variety of reasons, among which the most obvious are the authoritarian nature of the Catholic Church, its long history, its tremendous institutional organization, and the fact that its basic doctrines and philosophy are determined by persons residing in Italy and relatively immune from the influences of American values.

Yet even Roman Catholicism has not been unaffected by the processes of competition. Some changes have been within the framework of basic dogma and way of life; the puritanization of American Catholicism is the best illustration of this. Some have been within basic dogma but hardly consistent with tradition or philosophy; the espousal of extreme nationalism is an example. And some have even touched dogma and doctrine. I think that Catholic approval of the rhythm method of birth control is in some measure an accommodation to secular-humanist values. I think too that the thinking of persons like Father John Courtney Murray on the validity of religious liberty even in a Catholic state (a reflection of secular humanist influence) is likely to have an increasing effect within Catholicism as time goes on. The acceptance by American Catholicism of even a limited principle of separation of church and state despite earlier strong papal denunciations of that principle is clear evidence of the effect upon Catholicism of the cultural competition of the Protestant-humanist alliance. Moreover, even that limited interpretration implies a *de facto* equality of all faiths, itself a concept strongly denounced in Catholic doctrine. Roman Catholicism moves slowly, much more slowly than Protestantism or Judaism, but it does move.

COMPETITION AND AMERICA'S FUTURE

The most important consequence of competition has been the external changes effected by the competitors, the changes without themselves, the changes upon American cultural values and patterns. This book began with the recounting of such changes in one particular cultural institution, Christmas. Others indicated here have included the nature of Sunday observance, our moral standards as expressed in the penal codes, our family and welfare laws, our concepts of the relationship of church and state, our public school system, and many others. Upon each of these changes the various competing groups have in greater or lesser extent exercised some influence.

Today the most serious challenge to American cultural patterns and values fixed by a Protestant-humanist alliance comes from Roman Catholicism. That challenge has really just begun. In all likelihood it will be with us for a long time and will become increasingly stronger as time goes on.

Those committed to the validity of the patterns and values that evolved out of the Protestant-humanist alliance have no need to fear nor cause to complain. If their commitment is correct, the challenge will be successfully met and they can be grateful for the opportunity to vindicate their principles and values. If the challenge will result in some modification of the traditional American way of life, it can be safely assumed that the modification, if it lasts, will have been proved desirable and worthwhile; for American society is dynamic, not static, and competition among religious cultures is creative, not destructive. Unless American history is completely deceiving, it can safely be predicted that whatever does happen will justify the American experiment.

INDEX

Abolitionists, 69, 134
Age of Reason, The, 29
America (magazine), 13
American Christian Palestine Committee, 151
American Civil Liberties Union, 68, 70, 132, 142
American Commonwealth, The, 18
American Council for Judaism, 14, 150
American Council of Churches, 139
American Dilemma, An, 19
American Ecclesiastical Review, 40
American Ethical Union, 68
American Jewish Congress, 109, 132
American Jewish League Against Communism, 150
American Legion, 137
American Tract Society, 103
American Tragedy, An, 104
American Unitarian Association, 68
Amor Conjugalis, 104
Anglican Church and Anglicanism, 7, 9, 26–28, 36, 57, 59, 65, 88, 94, 109, 166
Antic Hay, 108
Anti-Federalists, 30
Anti-Saloon League, 97, 98, 109
Anti-Semitism, 33, 60, 78, 150, 151
Arab-Israel relations, 149, 150
Arabs, 151, 152
Armageddon, 159

Aryan race, 82
Augsburg, Peace of, 17
Augustine, St., 38

Baal, 159
Baby Doll, 95, 109
Backus, Isaac, 43
Baptist Church and Baptists, 26, 27, 42, 43, 65, 73, 105, 133
Beard, Charles, 97
Beard, Mary, 97
Beecher, Lyman, 29
Bible, 28, 29, 38, 48, 57–61, 65, 72, 73, 75, 124, 142, 156
Bible schools, 4, 67
Bill of Rights, 15, 28, 30, 40, 43, 142, 144
Bismarck, Chancellor Otto von, 17
Blake, Eugene Carson, 142
Blanshard, Paul, 61, 157
Book of Sports, 94
Boston, 1, 100, 131
Boston, Archdiocese of, 13, 100, 109
Boston Jewish Community Council, 109
Bower, Prof. William C., 71
Brethren, 143
Brooklyn, Archdiocese of, 13, 130
Bryce, Lord James, 18, 43, 47

Cabell, James B., 104

Index

Caldwell, Erskine, 108
California, Protestant Episcopal Diocese of, 115
Calvin, John, 39
Calvinism and Calvinists, 25–28, 32, 36, 42, 58, 65, 94, 95, 103, 105, 108, 109, 113, 114, 154
Canada, 136
Canon Law, 62, 107, 110, 118, 156
Canterbury, 139
Casti Connubi, 117
Cathedral of St. John the Divine, 115
Catholic Center Party, 164
Catholic Dictionary, 40, 41
Catholic Encyclopedia, 100
Catholic Hospital Association, 118
Catholicism in America, 107
Catholic News, 136
Catholic Party, 18
Catholic Principles of Politics, 37
Catholic Review, Baltimore, 136
Catholic War Veterans, 33, 107
Catholic Worker, 13
Central Conference of American Rabbis, 135
Central-Verein, 134
Champaign, Ill., 67, 68
Chase, Rev. J. Franklin, 104, 105
Chicago, Ill., 70
Chicago, University of, 71
Child Labor Amendment, 6
Christian Center Party, 18
Christian Century, The, 143, 151
Christian Democrat Party, 164
Christian Heritage, 61
Christianity and Crisis, 143
Christian Science Church and Christian Scientists, 73, 119, 122
Christ, Jesus, 2, 3, 17, 34, 42, 61, 112, 124, 143, 159, 166
Christmas, 1–6, 20, 72
Church and State (a periodical), 73
Church Lobbying in the Nation's Capital, 98

Churchman, The, 151, 166
Church Peace Union, 142
Civilta Cattolica, 37, 41
Clark, Gen. Mark W., 148
Cleveland, Ohio, 118
Cochran v. Louisiana State Board of Education, 90, 91
Cohn, Roy, 141
Colombia, 146
Common Sense, 45
Commonweal, 13, 107, 137
Communist China, 146
Comstock, Anthony, 103, 105
Comstock Law, 114
Conant, James Bryant, 79
Confessions, 104
Congregational Church and Congregationalists, 5, 7, 9, 26, 27, 57, 64, 65, 88, 154, 166
Congress, 48, 49, 52, 54, 67, 144
Connecticut, 103, 118, 162, 164
Conservative Judaism, 54, 102, 135
Constantine, 125
Constitutional Convention, 45–46
Converted Catholic Magazine, 61
Coughlin, Rev. Charles, 11
Council of Trent, 125
Cromwell Period, 103
Crowley, Francis M., 77
Crusaders, 160
Cubberly, Elwood P., 64

d'Alembert, Jean, 29
Declaration of Independence, 30, 45, 48
Democratic Convention, 11
Deuteronomy, 103
Dougherty, Cardinal Denis J., 106
Dred Scott decision, 69
Dreiser, Theodore, 104
Duluth, Minn., 106

Easter, 4, 72
Eastern Orthodox Churches, 32, 34

Ebersole, Luke, 98
Educational Policies Commission, 71
Egypt, 151
Eighteenth Amendment, 6, 94, 96, 97, 98
Eisenhower, President Dwight D., 51, 137
Elijah, 159
Ellises, 128, 132
Elmer Gantry, 104
England, 94, 136
Episcopalian Church and Episcopalians, 7, 26–27, 34, 42, 65, 97, 166
Essenes, 96
Eve of All Saints, 159
Everson v. Board of Education (Everson case), 47, 52–55, 67, 75, 76, 88, 90, 91
Everson-McCollum principle, 49–51, 53, 54

Farrell, James T., 108
Federal Anti-Lottery Law, 100
Federal Civil Aeronautics Authority, 98
Federal Council of Churches, 114, 134
Fifth Amendment, 141
Finaly Case, 128
Fine, Gov. John S., 130
First Amendment, 17, 43, 44, 46, 48–55, 65, 67, 68, 74, 88, 90, 148
Fitch, Florence Mary, 156, 157
Fitzgerald, Msgr. Thomas J., 106
Florida, 128, 131
Florida Catholic, 136
Fordham University, 77
Forever Amber, 106
Forney, Rev. Melvin M., 93
Fourteenth Amendment, 55, 90
France, 61, 108, 128
Frankfurter, Justice Felix, 94
French Enlightenment, 9, 29, 103, 163
French Revolution, 9, 59, 137

Friends, 143
Fundamentalist Protestantism, 141

General Conference of Seventh Day Adventists, 68
Genius, The, 104
German Catholics, 134
German language, 83
Germany, 21, 35
Ghetto, 59
Gibbons, Cardinal James, 100
God's Little Acre, 108
Goldman Case, 127–28, 130, 132
Good Friday, 4, 5
Gordon, Janet Hill, 123
Gordon-Peterson Bill, 124
Grant, President U. S., 67
Great Awakening, 27
Great Britain, 143, 150

Hager, Don J., 159
Hanukkah, 3, 4
Harper's Magazine, 107
Harriman, Gov. Averell, 102
Hemingway, Ernest, 104, 108
Hennings, Sen. Thomas C., Jr., 54
Henry, Patrick, 88
Herberg, Will, 53
"Hildy" Case, 128, 131, 132, 155
Hill-Burton Act, 117
Hitler, Adolf, 150
Hoban, Archbishop Edward F., 118
Holland, 1
Holmes, John Haynes, 95
Holmes, Justice Oliver Wendell, 15, 120
Holy See, 149
Hoover, Herbert, 98
House Committee on Un-American Activities, 139
House of Representatives, U. S., 158
Human Growth (film), 121
Human Reproduction (film), 121
Hungary, 145

Hutchinson, Ann, 9
Huxley, Aldous, 108

"In God We Trust," 49
Inquisition, 38, 39
Iowa, 83
Ireland, 10, 95, 108, 150
Isherwood, Christopher, 108
Islam, 160
Israel, State of, 14, 41, 42, 148–52
Italy, 109, 137

Jackson, Justice Robert, 75, 76, 77
James I, 94
Japanese-American School, 84
Jefferson, Thomas, 30, 43, 47, 54, 58, 64, 88, 96
Jehovah's Witnesses, 160, 161
Jersey City, N.J., 119
Jerusalem, 152
Jesuits, Order of, 37, 41
Jesus: See Christ, Jesus
Jewish religious schools, 90
Joint Baptist Committee on Public Affairs, 68
Journal of Social Issues, The, 159
Joyce, James, 104
Jurgen, 104
Justice and Judaism, 135

Kennedy, John F., 11
Kerr, Walter, 107
Know-Nothings, 10, 20, 61, 66
Korean War, 143, 145
Kreutzer Sonata, 104
Ku Klux Klan, 10, 11

Lateran Agreements, 95
Lawrence, D. H., 108
Legion of Decency, 106, 107, 108, 110
Lehman, Sen. Herbert H., 141
Leland, John, 43
Leo XIII, Pope, 37, 51
Letters from My Windmill, 108

Levittown, N.Y., 121
Lewis, Sinclair, 104
Life (magazine), 82
Lipman, Eugene, 135
Locke, John, 30, 45
London, 95
Look (magazine), 82
Lord, Bishop John Wesley, 131
Lord's Day Alliance, 55, 93, 104, 110
Loyalists, 27
Luther, Martin, 39, 159
Lutheran Church and Lutherans, 10, 21, 77
Lynn, Mass., 127

Maccabees, 3, 42
Mackay, John A., 142
Madison, James, 17, 39, 45, 46, 144
Magna Carta, 83
Mann, Horace, 64, 65
Maryland, 39
Massachusetts, 26, 43, 58, 100, 103, 109, 117, 127, 128, 130, 131
Massachusetts Bay, 1, 9
Massachusetts Civil Liberties Union, 109
Massachusetts Commission on Communism, 139
Massachusetts Council of Churches, 109, 131
Massachusetts Department of Public Welfare, 127
McCarthy, Joseph R., 11, 13, 136–37, 141, 142, 158
McCollum, Mrs. Vashti, 68
McCollum v. Board of Education (McCollum Case), 14, 52–55, 66–70, 73, 76
Memorial and Remonstrance, 46
Mennonites, 143
Methodist Board of Temperance, Prohibition and Morals, 97
Methodist Church and Methodists, 7, 26, 27, 65, 139, 143

Methodist Episcopal Church South, 97
Methodist General Conference, 143
Mexico, 61, 81
Meyer v. Nebraska, 83, 84
Michigan, 128
Middle East, 150
Mindszenty, Cardinal Joseph, 146, 147
Miracle, The (film), 16, 95, 108, 160
Miracle Case, 94
Missouri, 54, 132
Mohammed, 124
Moral and Spiritual Values in the Public Schools, 71
Moravian Church and Moravians, 28
Moses, 24, 124
Motion Picture Production Code, 106
Mount Carmel, 157
Murray, Rev. John Courtney, 40, 41, 107, 167
Myrdal, Gunnar, 19

Nana, 108
Nasser, President Gamal, 151
National Catholic Almanac, 78
National Catholic Welfare Conference, 52, 133
National Conference of Christians and Jews, 32, 155, 156, 157
National Council of Catholic Men, 107
National Council of Churches of Christ, 5, 33, 56, 69, 70, 73, 134, 139, 148, 166
National Educational Association, 71–72, 79
National Office for Decent Literature, 104, 106, 107, 108
National Organization for Decent Literature, 104
National Prohibition Party, 97
National Temperance Society, 97
Native Son, 108
Nativists, 10, 20, 61
Nativity, 1, 2

Nazi Occupation Forces, 128
Nazism, 142, 144
Nebraska, 83
Negro-White Relations, 19–21, 81
Netherlands, 87, 89
New Amsterdam, 1
New England Watch and Ward Society, 104, 106, 109
New Orleans, 125
New York, Archdiocese of, 70, 71, 106
New York Board of Rabbis, 71, 72, 73, 102, 123, 132
New York City, 15, 49, 62, 70–74, 95, 101, 111, 115, 123, 157, 164
New York Civil Liberties Committee, 111
New York Society for the Suppression of Vice, 103, 104, 106, 109
New York State, 16, 66, 102, 111, 123, 160
New York State Constitutional Committee, 132
New York State Council of Churches, 111, 123
New York State Roman Catholic Welfare Committee, 121, 123
Nicholas, St., 1
Niebuhr, Reinhold, 143
Ninety-five Theses, 159
NODL: See National Office for Decent Literature
Nordic race, 82

O'Connell, Cardinal, 100
Official Catholic Directory, 77, 101
O'Hara, Archbishop John F., 130
Ohio, 83
Old Testament, 72
One God—The Ways We Worship Him, 156
"On the Christian Education of Youth," 62, 76
Oregon, 83

Oregon Parochial School Case: See *Pierce v. Society of Sisters*

Orthodox Judaism, 34, 35, 42, 55, 115, 132, 135, 139

Outlaw, The, 106

Oxnam, Bishop G. Bromley, 115, 139, 142, 162

Paine, Tom, 29, 45

Paris, 95

Parkhurst, Charles H., 95

Parliament, 1, 143

Parochial Bus Case: See *Everson v. Board of Education*

Parochial Textbook Case: See *Cochran v. Louisiana State Board of Education*

"Parson's Case," 88

Passion plays, 4

Pearl Harbor, 143, 144

Pennsylvania, 128–29, 130

Peterson, Dutton S., 123

Pharisees, 159

Philadelphia, Pa., 18, 46, 106, 130

Pierce v. Society of Sisters, 83, 84, 86, 87

Pike, James A., 115

Pilot, The, Boston, 13, 100, 130

Pius XI, Pope, 50, 62, 76, 112, 116, 117, 119

Pledge of Allegiance, 31, 49, 51, 54

Poland, 21, 60, 61, 145, 146

Porgy and Bess, 21

Presbyterian Church and Presbyterians, 28, 45, 65

Primer on Roman Catholicism for Protestants, 105

Prohibition of intoxicating liquors, 7, 8, 27, 97–100

Protestant Council of New York, 71, 74, 111

Protestants and Other Americans United for Separation of Church and State, 20, 61, 73, 91, 132, 148, 155

Protocols of the Elders of Zion, 10

Providence, R.I., 13

Public Education in the U. S., 64

Puerto Rico, 81

Puritan Army Council, 143

Puritan Church and Puritans, 6, 9, 110, 154

Quakers, 9, 27, 39, 42, 133

Quebec, 87

"Red Dean," 139

Reform Judaism, 35, 54, 90, 102, 135, 144

Register Times-Review, La Crosse, Wis., 136

Religion in the Development of American Culture, 29

Restoration, English, 103

Revolutionary War, 27, 88, 164

Rise of American Civilization, 97

Rome, 95

Rommen, Heinrich, 40

Roosevelt, Mrs. Eleanor, 20, 162

Rosenberg, Ethel, 137

Rosenberg, Julius, 137

Rousseau, J. J., 29, 45, 104

Russia, 21, 60, 61

Russian Revolution, 137

Ryan and Boland, 37, 41

Sabbath, 4, 5, 48, 93, 95, 96, 99, 109–11, 134, 136, 138

Saracens, 160

Satan, 58

Saturday Evening Post, 82

Saudi Arabia, 40

Scandinavia, 21

Scriptures, 58

Seleucids, 42

Senate Committee on the Judiciary, 54, 56

Senate, U. S., 158
Seventh Day Adventists, 77, 111
Seward, William H., 66
Show Boat, 21
Shultz, Rabbi Benjamin, 141, 150
Sinai Peninsula, 149
Smith, Alfred E., 11
Society for the Reformation of Morals, 103
Society for the Suppression of Vice: See New York Society for the Suppression of Vice
Soviet Russia, 40, 43, 145–47
Spain, 38, 39, 146
Spanish Civil War, 137
Spellman, Cardinal Francis, 20, 95, 109, 136, 162
Statute Establishing Religious Freedom (Virginia), 46, 88
Stayman, Samuel, 43
Stepinac, Archbishop, 146, 147
Stockholm Peace Petition, 143, 144
Stuart aristocracy, 26
Stuber, Stanley, 105
Sun Also Rises, The, 104
Sunday Laws, 5, 14, 55, 56, 94, 99, 104, 109–11, 124
Supreme Court, United States, 14, 15, 19, 39, 47–49, 53–55, 67–69, 83–91, 104, 120–21, 127, 133, 161
Sweden, 41
Swedenborg, Emanuel, 104
Sweet, William Warren, 29
Switzerland, 41
Synagogue Council of America, 54, 68, 139
Syracuse, N.Y., 109
Syria, 151

Tablet, The, Brooklyn, 13, 130
Talmud, 24, 115, 124
Talmudic Judaism, 36, 59
Tariff Act of 1842, 103
Ten Commandments, 71, 72

Thanksgiving, 1, 2
Thirteenth Amendment, 96
Tidings, Los Angeles, 136
To Have and Have Not, 108
Tolstoy, Leo, 104
Torah, 24, 59
Trinity, 9
Tripoli, 29
Truman, Harry S., 16, 148
Tudor aristocracy, 26
Turks, 46

Ulysses, 104
Union of American Hebrew Congregations, 135
Unitarian Church and Unitarians, 27, 65, 73
United Arab Republic, 151
United Nations, 145
United Synagogue, 102
Universalist Church and Universalists, 27
Ursuline Convent, 125

Vatican, 95, 137, 145
Vatican, Ambassador to, 14, 31, 55, 56, 88, 148–49
Vermont, 103
Virginia, 64, 65, 73
Voltaire, Francois Marie Arouet de, 29
Vorspan, Albert, 135

Washington, D.C., 133
Watch and Ward Society: See New England Watch and Ward Society
Wells, H. G., 104
Williams, Roger, 43
Wise, Rabbi Stephen, 135
Wittenberg, 159
Women in Love, 108
Women's Christian Temperance Union, 97
Worcester, Mass., 110
World Council of Churches, 55

Index

World in the Evening, The, 108
World I Never Made, A, 108
World of William Clissold, The, 104
World War I, 2, 70, 82, 83, 144
World War II, 10, 142, 145
Wright, Bishop John J., 110
Wright, Richard, 108

Yale University, 29
Yearbook of American Churches, 5

Zionism and Zionists, 20, 150
Zola, Emile, 108
Zorach v. Clauson, 49, 69, 76, 77, 90